Leading with

Heart & Soul

TONI CHRISTIE

*This book is dedicated to my Dad
who was a kind and generous leader to so
many throughout his life.*

*Thank you for giving me a worthy set
of values and believing I could achieve
anything I wanted in this life.*

Rick Bettle
1947 - 2016

*Rest in peace my darling Da & know
that you will always be my hero.*

Contents

Foreword

Toni Christie has nailed it! She understands that mastering the technical skills of administration is not enough to become a respected leader of an early care and education programme. The values and beliefs that give life to a director's convictions and are lived through daily actions are what distinguish ordinary from extraordinary leaders.

Toni is certainly one of those extraordinary leaders in our field. She is unequivocal in the core values that serve as the foundation for her leadership role at Childspace. Her personal values shape her beliefs about what is important to pursue, how she treats others, and how she chooses to spend her time. Her message in Leading with Heart and Soul is that taking time to explore one's own values, beliefs, and deeply held principles is essential to leading with clarity and purpose. Put simply, directors' core values provide a moral compass about how to handle the myriad of issues that arrive at their doorstep every day.

Achieving clarity about one's personal values and beliefs is also an essential first step for guiding discussions with staff about the shared values that define organisational excellence and success. As Toni's leadership journey so clearly illustrates, this is not something that is accomplished in a single, hour-long staff meeting or one-day retreat. It is an ongoing process that takes place over months, even years. Leading with Heart and Soul reminds us what it means to lead with integrity so our rhetoric matches our actions. What a powerful message for both novice and seasoned directors.

Paula Jorde Bloom, PhD

Distinguished Professor of Research and Practice
Founder of the McCormick Center for Early
Childhood Leadership
National Louis University

Acknowledgements

This book has benefited greatly from the copy edit skills of Dr. Paula Jorde Bloom; the input of my long-time mentors Fay Clarke and Karen Stephens; the design genius of Jasmine Bailey; and the punctuation, grammar and spelling edits from my delightful mother in law, Catherine Christie and my super-smart daughter, Tui Christie.

Life has been brought to these pages by the images of many wonderful people young and old. I thank you all for recognising the great value of sharing these special moments and for capturing them so beautifully.

The other people in my life who I thank for their continued support and faith in my abilities to do bold things are my friends, colleagues, and family. Most especially you, Robin Christie, who makes all things good and lovely!

About the illustrations

The illustrations throughout this book are collaborative original artworks by Toni and Robin Christie. Robin sketches a beautiful outline from his very clever and original brain and Toni tangles within the outlines. They are holiday meditations.

Introduction

It has been more than 21 years since the Childspace journey began and in this time our team has learned so much about leadership and teamwork. After all this time, we feel like we've come to a place where we're leading each day with heart and soul. The point of this book is to share experiences from our years as leaders at Childspace Early Learning Centres and the Childspace Early Childhood Institute. Particularly, our successes – and even our mistakes – that helped build our early childhood organisation from one small home-based programme to four high-quality early learning centres, a thriving institute for adult learning, a workshop specialising in the design and construction of children's furnishings and equipment, and a family of people committed to a unified vision for young children and families.

In the following chapters I'll share ideas about leading with heart and soul. I'll illustrate them with quotes, graphics, images, and stories from experience. I encourage you to adapt anything that will be useful in your own context. Your instinct is the most powerful tool in your leadership box and every context, personality, and situation will determine the approach you take as a leader. There is no right answer and our best judgment is all there is; we do the best we can with the information we have at any given time.

Leadership and management are areas which require further exploration than is currently afforded in our formal teaching qualifications for early childhood. Our undergraduate qualifications focus solely on the skills and attitudes required for teaching in early childhood, yet there is no difference in qualifications required for teachers and managers in early childhood settings. Often, teachers are thrust into management positions well before they are mentally or emotionally prepared.

My aim in writing this book is to get people thinking about their own values as leaders. The twelve chapters I have written define and unpack the core values that have shaped my leadership and our organisation at Childspace. These examples will provide existing and potential leaders in early childhood with an outline of some of the personal values I have found to be effective and how these values relate practically and professionally to the leadership role. What do you value? It is worth exploring your core values in relation to leadership and ensuring they align with the values of your organisation and the team with whom you work and play.

The book's title "Leading with Heart and Soul" expresses what I think is required to lead a team in early childhood education. If your heart and soul aren't in it, then neither should you be. This book shares a values-based theory of leadership at Childspace which links to the same values we uphold, admire and display. I hope this approach will be of use in your work – from one leader to another.

A her-story: my personal journey in leadership

I always knew I wanted to work with children. One of my earliest memories is of playing for hours as the 'teacher' to my classroom set up in our garage where I had a group of very individual stuffed toys and dolls. I don't know if I had any natural skills in this regard as I recall being extremely judgmental, labelling certain of my toys and dolls as the 'naughty' ones. Certainly I had a passion for teaching, for leading, and for spending countless hours talking and 'listening' to these inanimate objects who would be my first learners.

For someone so interested in teaching and learning from a very early age, one might have expected that I'd be able to pay a little more attention in class. Not so. The parts of my education that I found by far the most rewarding were the sports, arts, socialising and one work placement at a local early childhood playgroup. My grades were average and my report cards were full of comments such as: "not realising her full potential due to being the class clown." It would be fair to say that school was not able to hold my attention, so school and I parted company under mutually amicable and fairly relieved terms after what used to be called sixth form (now year 12).

Living in Wellington, I was quite keen to get away from the town I had grown up in and fancied the idea of going to nanny school in Christchurch. This would be a grand and exciting adventure as it was in another city, I would be living in a flat, I would learn more about children, after the year of study I would be able to travel the world with my new nanny qualification, and develop my independence. So off I went to Rangi Ruru Nanny School where I would meet a singularly inspiring mentor, Norah Fryer.

Norah lit a fire in me that will burn brightly until the day I die. She opened my eyes to the importance of getting it right with our little people in their earliest years. When I got the message and asked Norah why she wasn't shouting this message from the top of the tallest mountain she replied with just a look. Her eyes, at the end of her career, said to mine, at the beginning of my career, "but I have been, and now it is your turn." It was sort of like a Yoda to Luke Skywalker moment - Norah sensed the force was strong in me.

And so I was hooked. I was to become, as many before me, a lifelong learner and advocate for this wonderful time of life we call early childhood. I embarked on further university study in psychology, sociology, human development and education. It was that year, at Canterbury University, that I met the love of my life, Robin – whom I wisely married.

I completed a second year of study under Norah's tutelage. This was a pilot programme which took off as the second year of Nanny training and was a course in how to set up and run an early childhood centre. Norah encouraged me towards a year of research after I had completed this new diploma and my position became one called the family facilitator.

As the only family facilitator involved in the project I would visit new young mothers and help them with whatever housework needed doing while subtly transferring essential messages about the care and education of their new baby. At the conclusion of this year of research I tried a few teaching roles in ECE services and kept up the friendships I had formed with the mothers I had met through my research.

I was frustrated by the run-down environments and some very suspect teacher practices at the centres where I worked. I would complain to Robin and to the mums I knew as a family facilitator and we all agreed that Robin and I should start our own early childhood centre. This would be in Shirley, Christchurch, an area central to the family facilitator programme and therefore an area where we could afford to buy a house and with an existing clientele of mums and babies with whom I had already established relationships. We needed to be sure we had a market ready to receive our services. Networking with clientele would be crucial to our projected success.

The bank accepted a business plan which had been written as a result of a "start your own small business" course I attended. With financial backing from my parents and the templates from my course with Norah (our biggest and most challenging assignment that year involved designing, equipping, licensing, and running an imaginary early learning centre), Robin and I were up and running our programme within nine months of purchasing our first home together.

We had a bedroom and our staffroom/office was also our lounge. The rest of the house was a preschool and we worked from seven in the morning until six at night five days a week for three years. It was a labour of love and we would usually also be working in the weekends on murals, playground improvements, administration, and tending to the multitude of animals we kept as part of the programme.

After three years of living, loving, playing, and working at Childspace in Christchurch we decided to move to Wellington where we would be closer to our parents so that our (as yet unborn) children could be closer to their grandparents.

The demand for good quality child care in Wellington was huge and we were able to open all four Childspace early learning centres within five years (1997-2001). We also gave birth to our two children, Max and Tui during this massive time of investment, growth, determination and hard-work!

As word of our centres, programmes, management and environments spread, so too did the visitors to our centres, the waiting lists, and the invitations to help other groups with their environment design, programme planning, management systems, and more. Our success in helping others in the field led directly to the development of our institute and workshop.

I completed my master's degree in 2011 and subsequently published my research into calm and nurturing infant care and education, and disseminated the research via a Fulbright Scholarship to the USA in 2013. My husband Robin has also developed an international reputation and contributed greatly to the field of early childhood design both indoors and out. In the last few years Robin and I have delivered keynote addresses, seminars, consultancy and workshops to parents and teachers all over New Zealand and Australia, as well as Canada, the Cook Islands, Denmark, Germany, Fiji, Ireland, Malaysia, Mexico, Scotland, Singapore, India, and the United States.

At the time of putting this book together our organisation employs more than seventy amazing people. We serve more than 200 families as well as thousands of early childhood centres and professionals in New Zealand and many other countries around the world. Our big dream at the moment is to establish an early learning centre with a strong nature focus on our ten acres at home. Our long term vision has always been to provide an undergraduate qualification in ECE because we believe the selection and initial education of our teachers is the best shot we have at creating excellent quality outcomes for children.

"*Courage is the first of human qualities because it is the one quality that guarantees all others.*" ~ Aristotle

Chapter 1:

Be courageous

To be truly courageous we have to be willing to have difficult conversations and approach conflict openly and honestly. There are useful models to help us with conflict resolution as well as giving and receiving feedback. We have to be honest with ourselves and others, be real, think creatively, trust our instincts, and back our vision with hard work and enthusiasm.

Leadership is not for the faint-hearted. If you think maybe you're not strong or brave enough to be a leader then run away now while you still can! Seriously. Don't even read another word. Quietly put the book down and find another job because leading a team in early childhood education requires courage.

We need courage to have difficult conversations, to feel empathy for others, to be vulnerable at times, to not always know the answers, to set a big vision, and to hold others accountable. Sometimes it takes a great deal of courage just to get to work on any given day!

Courage is the ability to confront our fears. We show courage when we are strong in the face of fear, grief or times of difficulty. Courage is displaying grace when under pressure and being brave enough to have potentially difficult conversations and embark on challenging projects.

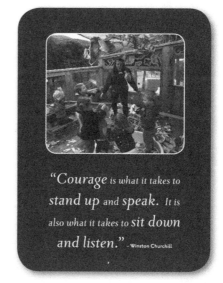

"Courage is what it takes to stand up and speak. It is also what it takes to sit down and listen." – Winston Churchill

COMMUNICATING WITH COURAGE

Unless we are courageous, we can easily fall into the trap of poor communication simply because we lack the courage to say what really needs to be said. When we don't apply courage to honestly confront a problem, we often resort to gossip that greatly undermines the chances for reasonable resolution.

One of the most frustrating paradoxes about leadership is that the things we find the most difficult are the things we often shy away from. For example, sometimes we avoid, delay or ignore conversations we need to have rather than confronting them. The paradox is that ONLY practice will improve our confidence to confront situations and our ability to get our point across succinctly, tactfully, honestly and graciously.

The following illustrates some ideas around communication do's and don'ts.

DO	DON'T
• Be totally honest. • Say what's on your mind even if it is a little thing. • Address your issues with the person they concern. • Listen carefully and value feedback. • Ensure you are all on the same page to create synergy.	• Just agree/avoid because it's easier/nicer. • Bottle up your worries. • Stab your colleagues in the back in passive aggressive ways such as sharing rumours. • Ignore what you don't like hearing or interrupt with excuses. • Head off on your own tangent without sharing your ideas.

DELIVERING FEEDBACK

In my travels delivering seminars on communication, camaraderie and conflict I have found the subject of delivering and receiving feedback to be difficult for many. I came across a simple model many years ago called the DESC model. The DESC model was developed by Sharon and Gordon Bower and is discussed more fully in their book, *Asserting Yourself.*

DESC STANDS FOR DESCRIBE, EXPRESS, SPECIFY, AND CONSEQUENCE

Describe – the behaviour causing concern

Explain – how this makes you feel

Specify – the behaviour you would rather have

Consequence – state the consequence

For example:

Jessica has been late for work often lately and the leader of her team really needs to address this before it becomes an issue for productivity and fairness to the other members of the team. Using the DESC model we might say:

I've noticed you arrived late for work today and yesterday (**describe the behaviour**)

I feel let down (**explain how it makes you feel**)

I'd rather you came to work a little early so you can put your things away (**specify the preferred behaviour**)

And so we can greet the children together and on time (**consequence**)

Following this model allows me to give feedback directly and succinctly. Before I found this model I think I had a tendency to waffle and probably not make nearly as clear a point.

RECEIVING FEEDBACK

Another essential skill in leadership is the ability to receive feedback. Usually leadership positions are offered to those people who demonstrate excellent knowledge and skills. This can sometimes confuse leaders into thinking they are the most knowledgeable and the most skilled - at everything! This is almost certainly not the case and the only way we can make improvements is by encouraging and acknowledging feedback from within our teams.

Feedback leads to collaboration and unity within a team. Encouraging and accepting feedback as the leader ensures we don't alienate other members of the team by acting like a 'know it all.' Here are some useful tips on receiving feedback.

- This is NOT personal – look at things constructively.
- Listen carefully and avoid interrupting.
- Try not to be dismissive with reasons or excuses.
- Say "thank you for your feedback".
- Be grateful for feedback – it will guide improvements for the benefit of all.
- Give yourself time to process the feedback before responding.
- Keep emotions in check but be honest and graceful about your feelings.

WHEN CONFLICT OCCURS

No one ever entered into early childhood because conflict rings their bell. If that were the case we'd have gone into law, politics, or community policing. We're a pretty peaceful bunch on the whole so it's not surprising we often shy away from conflict situations. However, we need to adjust our attitudes a little and get away from the idea that conflict is a bad thing. Conflict is neither good nor bad - it is important if we want to get things done. Sometimes when we think of the word conflict, we imagine war and/or winners and losers. We need to get over the word and the associated negative mind traps and get on with making conflict work for us.

Conflict is usually about perception versus reality. We all have different perceptions and these can sometimes cloud the facts of a situation. If we can deal with only the parties involved then we have a much greater chance of resolving the conflict in a mutually acceptable way – with the ultimate goal of a win-win solution.

Unfortunately our human nature will often get in the way by snubbing the party with whom we share the conflict and instead talking to any number of other friends and support people in our lives. Because these friends are there for support, and they've only heard our side of the story, they will most often agree with our perception, and reinforce our righteousness, thereby reinforcing our perception further, and making it more difficult to resolve the conflict.

At the same time, the other party has gone to their friends and support people and had exactly the same experience. So now there are virtually no more facts in the matter, just two extremely overblown righteous perceptions!

I've had a go at drawing a diagram of this scenario below:

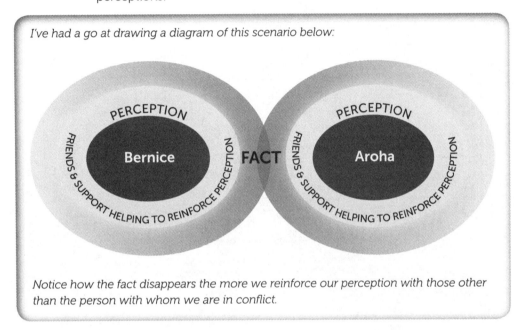

Notice how the fact disappears the more we reinforce our perception with those other than the person with whom we are in conflict.

It is best to avoid this situation by dealing with conflict openly, honestly, and as soon as possible. Most importantly, we really want to deal only with the parties involved if possible. To resolve conflict with courage, try following these simple steps:

- Do not blame – recognise the problem as being a joint issue.
- Try to keep feelings and perceptions separate from the facts.
- Define the problem and agree on it before moving on to resolution.
- Be clear and honest about feelings.
- Listen carefully to each other and don't interrupt.
- If you can resolve the conflict then you both win. Finding a win-win solution. may be easier than you think.

LET PEOPLE KNOW THE REAL YOU

Be courageous and let people know the real you. Who you are is who they will want to follow. There is real vulnerability in letting people know who you really are, what you believe in, who you love, what motivates you, and the various details that make up your character. Courageous leaders are open and honest about whom they really are. They are not trying to be someone they are not and this leads to a sense of openness and trust within the team.

"Qualities of a good leader – Self-belief; leads by example; integrity; accountability; action; risk-taker; guards energy; builds relationships; empowers others." ~ Fay Clarke

In the past (before I knew about the DESC model) I would tend to waffle when delivering feedback as this is my natural default setting when I'm nervous. This would mean I wasn't making my point clearly which would confuse the person to whom I was giving feedback – a waste of everyone's time and energy!

When I had to have a courageous conversation I'd often stay awake all night worrying how the other person might react to my feedback. I'd run through endless scenarios of "what if?" Once it came time to deliver the feedback I would be exhausted from lack of sleep, prepared for a million different "what if" scenarios, and still very nervous about our meeting. To my great surprise, I was finding that often the person to whom I was delivering the feedback would actually know that they needed to make improvements. Having rehearsed all the possible reactions in my head, the one I got most often was simply "I know." This has led me to understand that usually if someone is doing a poor job, they're actually aware of the fact on some level.

These days I employ courage every time I need to have a difficult conversation with a member of my team. I'm completely honest and most often start by saying "this is the least favourite part of my job." A very true statement that reassures my colleague that I'm not some kind of sadistic witch who actually enjoys delivering feedback someone might not want to hear. It also lets them know there's something possibly uncomfortable coming which provides a warning to be emotionally prepared.

Since I've been using the DESC model I find I am able to give feedback much more directly and promptly. I no longer take it home and replay it a million times in my head or lose sleep. I simply make my point succinctly, clearly, in a timely manner, and get on with it.

By far the best reaction to feedback I've ever had was from a colleague with whom I still work closely. After delivering her feedback regarding her performance at work, she agreed that she could make improvements and said "I'm sorry you had to do that. I know you don't like having to remind me things I should know better."

SIMPLE SUMMATIVE ADVICE

Communicate clearly, with empathy and honesty. Use a simple model like the DESC model to guide you and stop you from waffling or labouring the point when delivering feedback. Accept feedback as useful for self-improvements rather than interrupting with excuses or dismissing the feedback. Conflict is a natural and important part of growth. Accept it and deal with it quickly and clearly. Be your very best authentic self.

Dream big

" *Nothing happens unless first we dream.* "

~ Carl Sandburg

Chapter 2:

Dream big

Dreaming big is what distinguishes leadership (vision oriented) from management (task oriented). To dream big we must allow ourselves the time to day-dream, strive for excellence, avoid complacency, celebrate our achievements, employ initiative, and plan effectively. Strategic planning and self-review are effective tools for leaders to record and evaluate their process and progress towards achieving big dreams.

Excellence is the state or quality of excelling or being exceptionally good. Striving for excellence ensures we are not satisfied by mediocrity or complacent in the standards we set for ourselves.

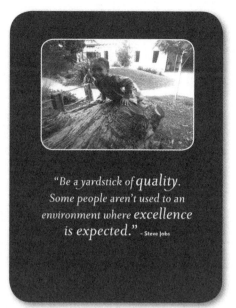

"Be a yardstick of quality. Some people aren't used to an environment where excellence is expected." - Steve Jobs

It is essential that members of our team know that we stand for excellence. Therefore we will expect more from our teams and the rewards will be greater because excellence creates motivation and satisfaction. There are plenty of average early childhood centres out there and these are the result of management, leadership and/or team members who are not prepared to go the extra mile to achieve excellence and pursue big audacious goals. Perhaps these people can be counselled into a career that doesn't require excellence for the benefit of children? Maybe grow flowers or trees but definitely not children!

"Managers do the thing right. Leaders do the right thing."

~ Warren G. Bennis

Vision is the big difference between management and leadership. Management is about deadlines, administration, tasks, procedures and measurements, whereas leadership is all about vision.

Leaders need to develop and share vision which comes from dreaming big. In order to dream big, we have to first allow ourselves the luxury of day-dreaming. When we invest the time in day-dreams our minds are truly free to journey through thoughts and experiences which make disparate connections that will result in the 'light-bulb' or 'aha!' moment that sows the seed of a big dream or vision.

Don't get me wrong. I'm pretty certain that no manager of an early childhood centre has time during their work day to sit around day-dreaming. These "aha!" moments are far more likely to occur in the shower or as we're dozing off to sleep.

" The mind in [a bored] state has no particular aim. It's not efficient or directed. It revisits experiences, scans for opportunities, plays with problems — and that's when creativity comes alive. These days, we rarely reach the point of boredom, thanks to gadgets and anytime, anywhere entertainment. Occupying our brains is too easy — and that's killing our creativity. When was the last time you rode an elevator and didn't pull out your phone? Every free moment has become an opportunity to get something done, or at least to be entertained. But doing nothing, being bored, is a precious thing. My best ideas come when I'm running without my iPod, simply sitting, or waiting for someone, or lying in bed before I go to sleep. These 'wasted' moments are the ones in which we most often unconsciously connect the dots."

~ Peter Bregman

SHARE YOUR VISION

A big dream or vision is entirely useless without the ability to share the vision. A vision must be introduced and promoted to others so that they might buy-in and become committed to what it is the organisation is hoping to accomplish. This buy-in is essential in leading and motivating others, and team members will be more inclined to support a vision they have been part of creating. This requires creativity and constant innovation. Leaders in early childhood must aim for the stars and yet have their feet firmly embedded in the sandpit.

Sharing vision means opening it up to interpretation and change within your team. I have met leaders who want their vision to remain pure and therefore ask team members to follow their vision without having offered them the opportunity to really buy-in, affect, or feel ownership of the plan. There is no surer way to fail. Unless all members of the team believe in and feel ownership of a vision then it has no value and is unlikely to be realised.

Sharing your vision means you are able to get everyone's great ideas and further strengthen the short and long-term goals of the organisation.

None of us is as smart as all of us

THE SEVEN P'S OF PLANNING

Of course, all these big dreams and shared visions mean nothing if we cannot execute them. This is where we need to take into account the seven P's and where the skills of management (planning) work hand in hand with the art of leadership (vision). My cousin Moosh, who was once in the army, taught me the seven P's:

Proper prior planning prevents piss-poor performance

A great leader plans to succeed and this must be done in increments rather than expecting everything to happen at once. Planning might be as small in scale as using our diary properly by setting tasks for each day and crossing them off as they are accomplished. Planning on a large scale would be writing five-year strategic plans for the direction of an organisation.

Anything we plan requires careful attention to detail. This is the case whether a project is small or large in scale, or whether it involves many others or just a few. When, what, and who will be the guiding questions in most cases when it comes to project planning. Highlighting individual responsibilities for each part of the plan and giving accurate timeframes to the actions required. It is the task of the leader to ensure all participants in the plan clearly understand their roles and responsibilities and buy-in – or commit to – the vision for the timely completion of any big dreams.

STRATEGIC PLANNING CREATES THE BIG PICTURE

A strategic plan is a document used to communicate an organisation's goals, the actions needed to achieve those goals, and what indicators exist to measure our progress toward reaching the stated goals. A strategic plan is a long term vision for an organisation – usually three to five years. It sets out the strategy and direction for the organisation, sets priorities, and ensures the team is working toward common goals.

Strategic plans are future-focused and should be regularly reviewed to ensure they are relevant, understood, and used as guiding documents. They usually consist of a vision, a mission, and goals. Plans can be linked to relevant regulatory or quality framework criteria depending on legislation or best practice governing your particular service.

STRIVING FOR CONTINUOUS IMPROVEMENT & SELF-REVIEW

Pursuing big dreams means consistently striving to achieve greater outcomes for children, families, our environment, and teaching teams. It can be tempting to rest on our laurels once we have achieved one goal or other but great leaders never let their vision stand still for long. As they make small improvements over time, they adjust their expectations and make strides towards even greater accomplishments. While this is a warning against complacency, it is also important to remember to celebrate both the small and more significant milestones along the way!

Self-review is a process for quality improvements which enables teachers to work collaboratively towards a shared vision for their organisation. It is a process that helps us evaluate the effectiveness of what we do, with the aim of improving the quality of our practice. In effective review, we take time to draw together the ideas of all members of our learning community. Each self-review cycle is a short to medium term plan (3-6 months) which works towards the vision, mission, and goals of the strategic plan.

We have developed a successful model of self-review at Childspace which takes us through the following steps:

Choose a topic for review: This might be an aspect of the day that feels frustrating, or it might be because we have new research in the field. We might want to make further improvements or address inconsistencies within the programme or teaching team.

This point in the process has us deciding as a team:

1. What is happening now?
2. What is the effectiveness of what is happening now?
3. What do we want to happen?
4. How would this improve our effectiveness?
5. What will we commit to?

Document our actions: This is where we provide evidence of our actions and decisions using photos, newsletters, and other modes of communication to provide the evidence of how, what, where, when, and who was involved.

Now we can look at the documentation of the process and decide:

1. Were there any trends and patterns?
2. What did we actually do?
3. Who was responsible?
4. How, where, and when? Do we have photos, newsletters, displays, courses attended, parent evenings, relevant readings and handouts we can include in the documentation?

Reflect on the learning and improvements: This may include team discussions, parent perspectives, children's voices, and research. We can discuss and celebrate successes, inconsistencies, or further explore possible options to try.

Upon reflection we can ask ourselves:

1. Did we do what we said we were going to do?
2. What did we notice/learn along the way?
3. What would we like to do/happen in the future?
4. What was the effectiveness of our actions?
5. Was there an increase in quality for children, parents, and teachers?
6. When will we plan to revisit?

Revisit the topic: Discuss how it is working a few months on. By revisiting a previous review focus we can decide whether there are any further considerations and whether we have made sustainable improvements.

When we revisit we can ask ourselves:

1. Is it as effective as first thought?
2. Are there further improvements to be made?
3. Are there any new trends and patterns?
4. Is it time to review this focus again?

Everything we have created at Childspace was a big dream once! Each early childhood service, our institute, our workshop, various publications and every new conference or professional development seminar was once just a big dream.

Right now our big dream is to open a nature school on the land next to our workshop. So far we have just been dreaming and scheming. Many ideas are being shared within a 'think-tank' of interested stakeholders, visionaries, and people with the complementary skills required for turning the dream into eventual reality.

At this stage we have deliberately not invited any accountants or bankers to day-dream with us as this could shatter our blue-sky visions with silly old reality. I think this is an important step because day-dreaming and budgets don't always go together. In time we will get into the planning, strategic planning, self-review, and the accounting can come into play at this point. This will no doubt refine our plans somewhat but it will ensure that we start with a big dream that can be realised with a little financial reality rather than starting with financial reality and feeling we are too restricted to dream big!

It might be five or ten years from now but one day children will have the opportunity to attend a Childspace nature school. This will be just ten minutes from our capital city and folks will come from all over the world to see this model of early childhood education in action!

SIMPLE SUMMATIVE ADVICE

Stand for excellence – this will attract like-minded educators who are fully committed and motivated to achieve the highest quality outcomes for children and their families. This will mean constantly striving for quality improvements through strategic planning and self-review. Take some time to day-dream. It is the dreaming, or vision, that separates leadership from management. Your ability to get everyone on board with a vision will depend on how much input they have had in shaping the vision. Getting from vision to reality requires very careful planning and execution.

Serve others

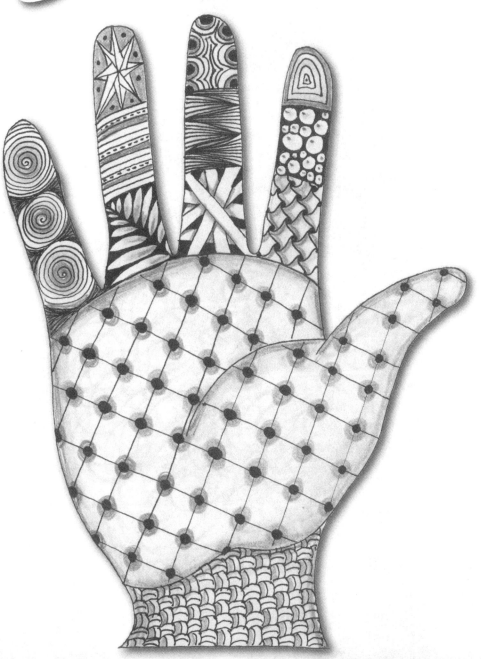

"Clients do not come first. Employees come first. If you take care of your employees, they will take care of the clients." ~ Richard Branson

Chapter 3:

Serve others

Leaders require a generosity of spirit that makes service a natural partner to leadership. Our generosity of spirit and willingness to serve provide a model for our team who will be more likely to exhibit generous tendencies by simply following the leader. We need to ensure we are super organised and willing to put the needs of our teachers first so they can be fully and happily engaged with the children.

Service is an act of giving. Service is giving something of ourselves for the benefit of others. When we serve others we show humility and empathy for the needs and desires of other living beings.

"The best way to find yourself is to lose yourself in the service of others."

– Mahatma Gandhi

I love the Bob Dylan lyric:

"everybody's got to serve somebody."

It is true. Have a think about it. In early childhood we are serving children and families while the parents who use our service are off serving others in their work. Even when we are at play or home we are serving. A coach serves the players; players serve supporters. When you last cleaned your house you were serving others in your household. On and on the list continues until you find that Dylan was exactly right. Everybody's got to serve somebody. Leaders have to serve the members of their team.

WHAT ARE OUR PEOPLE PRIORITIES?

I believe there are many principals or centre managers who will tell you that the children come first. I think this is a naïve or sentimental statement to make as a manager because in such a position your teachers must always come first! Teachers are unable to put the children first unless they have someone taking care of their needs. The needs of teachers can be found in the strands and goals of Te Whāriki (our national early childhood curriculum in New Zealand). They must feel a sense of well-being within the environment, they must feel that they belong, have a right to contribute, have the ability to communicate, and their exploration can be directly linked to professional development opportunities.

The emotional milestones for children developed by Erik Erikson demonstrate similarities for appropriate management practices. It is a leader's job to communicate and form basic trust with his or her teachers. A leader must also encourage and allow autonomy, and reward initiative and industry.

A good leader can create an environment where teachers are enjoying themselves, synergy is created and there is a feeling of respect, equality, tolerance, passion and enthusiasm. This does not happen when a manager puts the children first, it happens when they put their teachers first. They, in turn, put the children first, and in my experience whenever children are happy, the parents will always be happy.

The principal at Childspace has to put her centre managers first. She needs to ensure their needs are being met. They must be able to trust and confide in our principal, and we must be able to work as a team where the sum of the parts is greater than the whole. This synergy will have a direct effect on the health and well-being of the organisation as a whole. Managers are then able to put their teachers first, ensuring their needs are met and they are able to trust their leader, and work as a group towards ensuring the best possible outcomes for children. Each teacher is responsible for their own group of children – for whom they are primary caregiver; they must put the needs of this group first, ensuring they experience trust, respect, passion, enthusiasm, tolerance, belonging, well-being, communication, contribution, and exploration. A good teacher can deliver these gifts when the management structures and philosophies of an organisation are sound.

Be your teacher's primary caregiver so he or she can go off and be peaceful and engaged with children. As a leader it is important that you put your teacher's needs first. When they are acknowledged and supported in their roles, they will be able to put the children's needs first.

"We make a living by what we get.
We make a life by what we give."
~ Sir Winston Churchill

SERVING OTHERS REQUIRES A GENEROSITY OF SPIRIT

Leaders require a generosity of spirit. Remembering birthdays, allowing teachers to finish early when appropriate, bringing dinner or a bottle of wine to a meeting, cooking a meal for the team, covering a late or early shift for someone when required – these are all examples of generosity of spirit which will not only endear us to our team, but also sets an example of generosity for other team members to follow.

As with teaching, role-modelling is essential to good management and leadership. If we are admired, trusted and respected, our behaviour will be emulated by those around us.

So we must practice what we preach! Answer honestly, show up on time, keep promises, practice confidentiality, model basic trust and respect, and share knowledge.

ORGANISATIONAL SKILLS ARE A NON-NEGOTIABLE REQUIREMENT!

Excellent organisational skills are essential for effective and efficient management in early childhood settings. With a team of teachers, the demands of parents, and several small groups of children, there are always routines, rosters, spaces, breaks, meals, activities, and many other essential components to organise. The smooth running of any early childhood centre is attributable to its leader. While others in the team may take responsibility for certain organisational tasks, it is the leader who delegates these tasks and shows initiative in developing or reviewing systems to ensure their efficacy. The leader also takes responsibility on a daily basis for simple organisational systems such as day books, attendance registers, noticeboards for parents and staff, phone and email messages, correspondence, and much more. These tasks go unnoticed when they are done correctly but create enormous frustration for staff and parents if they are not.

"In the heart of every caregiver is a knowing that we are all connected. As I do for you, I do for me" ~ Tia Walker

PARALLELS BETWEEN TEACHING AND MANAGING

I believe there are many parallels that can be drawn between effective teaching in early childhood and effective management of teams of adults.

"If young children were always acquiescent and compliant, always able to control their impulses and interact competently, they would not, by definition, need the presence of knowledgeable and competent adults!" ~ Katz & McClellan

It could be argued that if teachers were always acquiescent and compliant, always able to control their impulses and interact competently, they would not, by definition, need the presence of a knowledgeable and competent leader!

This comment is certainly not meant to be patronising or belittling, it is simply an observation that children and adults are similar in their needs in that we are all human beings. I could be two or seventy-two but I still need to feel loved and respected. We strive for independence yet as social beings we never will be.

More parallels can be drawn between basic teaching strategies and effective management such as allowing autonomy in decision making, valuing input, respecting diversity, delivering appropriate praise and rewards, developing trust and consideration. The list goes on. When we act on behalf of others or advocate for them, we are serving them.

I wrote the following list more than ten years ago now and unearthed it while researching for this book. It still rings very true to me and relates most directly to the idea that we are serving others when we lead.

IF YOU WANT TO LEAD AN E.C.E. SERVICE BE PREPARED TO:

- Work longer and harder than the rest of your team. Nothing gains you respect like this will.

- Spend most of your time praising, encouraging, and reassuring your staff but don't expect to receive any in return.

- Be given a different story by every person regarding the same issue and wade through these in search of the truth.

- Spend time with your team as a teacher. This ensures:
    1. You lead by example.
    2. You know what is going on.

- Take paperwork home, work late, start early, spend weekends displaying work, cleaning the art room, re-arranging the block corner, etc.

- Admit when you are wrong.

- Handle difficult and sensitive situations professionally and confidentially.

- Have your patience tested more than you ever did as a teacher. Adults can be so much more trying than children.

- Fill in for any teacher at any time.

- Be an advocate for your teachers; you are their representative to parents, management, and community.

- Involve your teachers in decision making and let them know what is going on.

- Delegate responsibility. This ensures you do not get bogged down with extra work. More importantly it makes the teacher to whom you have delegated feel they are an important part of the team.

- Learn how to get the most out of your teachers. It will be different for each individual.

- Put your teachers first. If they are happy the children will be happy. If the children are happy the parents are always happy.

- Feel guilty about every minute you spend in the office as opposed to with your team but recognise the need to spend that time.

- Laugh — at yourself, with others, and whenever you can. Studies have shown people who laugh more are less stressed. Never underestimate the power of a sense of humour for getting you out of a difficult situation.

- Smile and bring chocolate.

OUR LEADERSHIP POTENTIAL IS DETERMINED BY THOSE CLOSEST TO US

John Maxwell would refer to the above description of management as the "law of the inner circle." He is alluding to delegation and leadership in manageable group sizes. For example, I could not possibly hope to know my whole team of seventy people in the ways that I know my management team of nine. Each of these leaders has their own team, and each of the teachers in their team has their own group of children. This "law of the inner circle" ensures each leader is working with an inner circle which is manageable.

Once upon a time....

We found an excellent way to build camaraderie that was almost entirely dependent on our ability to serve our team. We would essentially throw a party for our management team and their partners quite regularly at our house. We would serve a big dinner for everyone to begin with and then I would host the managers in the lounge and the 'First Husbands' Club' would convene in the garage with Robin. Our meeting had liquid refreshments and lots of team-building opportunities and Robin's 'First Husbands' Club' was open to any partner a centre manager might like to bring along – their status as husband, male, or actual partner held no relevance whatsoever. The First Husbands Club had a charter and specialised in playing silly games. Our management team would be able to discuss any issues without time constraints and once we were finished we were always pleased to join the partners in their games.

I will remember these events forever as some of the best parties we have ever hosted! We still have our managers' meetings and First Husbands Club these days. Now we are a bit older we host them as special twice annual rituals, as opposed to the monthly parties we used to throw.

Then and now, this is an obvious and enjoyable way we are able to serve our team as leaders. It demonstrates our gratitude and care, and cements our loyalty and generosity of spirit. Our service also provides a model to the leaders in our organisation which is replicated when they host their own teams for other events.

SIMPLE SUMMATIVE ADVICE

Generosity is a character trait of the best leaders. Your ability to model a generosity of spirit will set an example and endear you to your team. You need to ensure you are working closely with a manageable group in order to set the direction and vision of your organisation. In a stand-alone service this will probably mean your whole teaching team, but in leadership positions in larger organisations this may mean your head teachers, centre managers, regional co-ordinators or perhaps governing boards. Having a good sense of fun and humour and bringing chocolate is also an integral part of serving others!

Have empathy

"There is no wasted time when it is time spent building relationships."

Chapter 4:

Have empathy

To have empathy we need to suspend our judgment so we can truly see from another perspective. We need to spend time getting to know the individuals in our team and deliver feedback and/or delegate tasks according to their strengths and preferences. We need to listen, value, and meet the needs of our team members. Finally, we must be courageous about making the best decisions for the whole organisation, and have the best possible outcomes for children at the core of our actions and decisions.

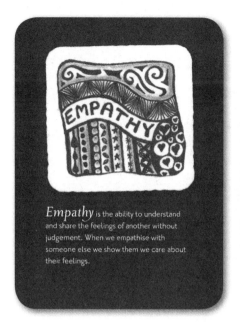

Empathy is the ability to understand and share the feelings of another without judgement. When we empathise with someone else we show them we care about their feelings.

"The great gift of human beings is that we have the power of empathy." – Meryl Streep

When we talk about empathy we often mention the idea of walking a mile in someone else's shoes. I once heard someone suggest you should walk a mile in your enemy's shoes – because by then you'll be a mile away from them and you'll have pinched their shoes!

Joking aside, we certainly can benefit from putting ourselves metaphorically in someone else's shoes because everybody has a story. I need to remind myself of this when I feel let down, angry or upset by someone's actions. We have to be disciplined and suspend our judgement in order to truly see things from another's perspective. This is the essence of empathy.

INVEST TIME IN GETTING TO KNOW PEOPLE

We need to invest time in really getting to know the people in our team so we can develop the kind of camaraderie and highly functional interpersonal relationships that will enable team members to empathise readily with one another.

When we can feel empathy for another, we are able to present information or ideas in ways that will best suit that individual person. This will differ between team members. For example, some people require almost constant praise or reassurance that they are doing a good job. For others this may seem over the top and make them uncomfortable. Some team members want feedback very directly and succinctly where others might need to hear some positive praise before they are able to hear constructive advice.

"The secret to change is to focus all of your energy, not on fighting the old but on building the new." ~Socrates

CHANGE IS CONSTANT

It has been said that the only person who likes change is a baby with a dirty nappy. But change is absolutely constant in early childhood settings. It is possibly the only consistent thing! Staff turnover happens for a variety of reasons out of your organisation's control. For instance, staff travel, childbirth, or moving to a different town. All impact a programme's ability to function. Even when the personnel in a centre remain stable over many years, there are still constant changes in regulations, environment, policy, and accountability measures. So change is something the best leaders get used to and learn to celebrate early on in their careers.

It is the leader who will set the tone for how everyone deals with change. When we lead an organisation that is constantly striving for improvement, then change is welcomed as a necessary part of making improvements. In order to feel positively about change, teams need the opportunity to share, discuss, and agree on plans that will ensure any change is positive for everyone involved. Team members will also need a leader who models optimism and positivity regarding change, and can empathise with team members regarding their feelings about change. We need to be very aware of the messages we are conveying via our attitude and body language.

BE MINDFUL OF INDIVIDUAL TEMPERAMENTS

Just as every child has an individual temperament, so does each adult. An intuitive and empowering leader will be mindful of the individual temperaments within his or her team. To inspire and empower we need to be constantly aware of, and responding to, individual temperament traits. For example, someone who is naturally anxious may require more support when implementing change.

EMPATHY AND THE BIGGER PICTURE

While we can empathise with another person, we must also recognise what is essential to the best outcomes for children, families, and other members of the team. For example when a member of our team is facing big personal issues we can understand, act compassionately, and sympathise, but still not allow these issues to negatively impact the programme and personnel for any longer than necessary. As the leader, we have to make decisions that require empathy as well as courage. This could mean suspending, warning or firing a team-member when they are emotionally vulnerable which seems like the opposite of empathy. However, we always have to act with the bigger picture in mind – the picture which includes all the children, families, and teachers our organisations serve.

When we show empathy for the person with whom we are addressing issues, we really need to think things through from their perspective and try to come to the best possible resolution for everyone. For example, we might offer some time away from work so that the issues can be resolved and therefore no longer impact our work environment. We might offer help from an external agency more appropriate to deal with the situation; we might suggest less responsibility or hours as a short-term solution; or we may need to summon all our tact to lay the situation out honestly as one that is untenable for its negative impact on others in the environment. In other words, having empathy for a team member doesn't always mean we have to accommodate them. The leader must do what is best for the team success rather than just one individual's preference or pleasure.

The first person I ever had to ask to leave our employ convinced me that I shouldn't. Seriously, I was all prepared for my courageous conversation but felt an intense amount of empathy for the person and really put myself in her shoes. My empathy stopped me from doing the right thing and trusting my instincts and I didn't let that teacher go when I should have. Six months later, when she had really done some damage to the culture and reputation of our organisation, I did what I should have done in the first place.

I learned a few valuable lessons from that situation:

1. *Always trust your instincts.*

2. *Empathy is a powerful tool to help us understand another person, present things to them so they will understand and take action, and develop respectful relationships. It can also stop us from doing the right thing for the organisation as a whole when we feel so much empathy for an individual whose behaviour is counter-productive to the goals of the organisation.*

3. *People look to the leader to take decisive action when it is required. How well a leader is respected within an organisation will depend on how willing they are to tackle the difficult tasks in order to benefit the group as a whole.*

SIMPLE SUMMATIVE ADVICE

Empathy is simply the ability to feel *with* other people. To develop empathy you must first invest time in getting to know members of your team. This will help you understand, without judgment, where they are coming from. Change is the only constant thing in early childhood environments and this will mean empathising with the anxieties and tensions team members feel about change. This chapter has outlined the pitfalls of having too much empathy. Respectful relationships that are warm, empathetic and caring are absolutely paramount to the culture of an organisation. However, leaders must also beware of making a poor decision because they feel empathy for one individual over the health of the whole organisation.

Foster loyalty

"Respect is earned, honesty is appreciated, love is gained and loyalty is returned."

Chapter 5:

Foster loyalty

Fostering loyalty helps to ensure consistency within our teams. That means we can have sustained focus, get the whole team on board with plans, and keep the team together as it heads towards its goals. When people have contributed and helped to shape a vision they have ownership, and are far more motivated to achieve results and to remain loyal to an idea and group. When team members feel rewarded and can see a clear career progression, they are more likely to remain loyal to an organisation.

Loyalty is belief, trust and dedication to a person or cause. We show loyalty when we support goals, ideals and outcomes that are mutually beneficial through a shared sense of honesty, trust and forgiveness.

"And we are loyal, keep it that way." – Dave Dobbyn

THE TEAM THAT PLAYS TOGETHER STAYS TOGETHER

People are loyal to their workplace only when they enjoy it. The most effective way we can help create a harmonious and enjoyable workplace is to work on camaraderie within the team. Camaraderie means highly functional interpersonal relationships and this means not only knowing each other and caring about each other, but also recognising that we are relying on each other to succeed as a team. In competitive situations others are hoping to see you fail, whereas in collaborative situations others are depending on you to succeed.

Sometimes we have to help team members with their understanding and practice of collaboration because all through our education system we have been set up to compete rather than collaborate. For example, exams, the bell curve, and almost every part of formal education sees us compared to each other and encourages us to compete in order to succeed. Upon release from the education system and despatch into the workforce we are suddenly expected to understand and work collaboratively. So we need plenty of opportunities to practice collaboration; luckily these team building ideas can also create joy for our teams.

The examples over the next two pages are team building ideas for early childhood centres.

The Great Race

On a teacher only day or a Saturday you gather your team (lots of prep and a decent budget will make this a huge success that will be remembered by the team forever). You divide your team into groups however you think works well, and each group has a passport. The idea is that they cross the borders of several countries as they trip around your neighbourhood (getting the help of friends and neighbours who live within walking distance is also crucial to the success).

Each location is a different 'country' and the team has to create/make/prepare/do something at each location within the allocated time (usually around 30 minutes at each station is sufficient) before the person in charge of the station is able to stamp their passport and send them off to their next destination.

Examples of activities for the country stations are:

- Make mocktails and cocktails for the evening entertainment that follows.
- Pitch a tent (for those staying later).
- Design and decorate a canvas/bunting/collage (materials prepared earlier).
- Prepare a chant/skit/dance/song/ ready to present to the larger group later.
- Collect flowers and create a wild flower bouquet along the walk/talk.
- Prepare dinner or dessert (ingredients all prepared earlier and full clean up completed before the passport is stamped).
- Assemble some kind of sculpture/woodwork/den.

The challenges at the stations are limited only by the imagination of the great race designer – YOU!

Secret squirrel

One of the most basic exercises that might be of use for some teams or leaders wanting to get to know their teams better I call 'secret squirrel'.

This involves each member of the team completing a page of information about themselves which lists their favorite food, drink, animal, movie star, singer, colour, etc. (more or differing favourites may be used).

The papers are then placed into a hat and each team member takes one out until all members of the team have someone else's information sheet. For the next fortnight team members have to sneak around secretly treating the person whose information they ended up with.

Everyone gets treats for a fortnight, much hilarity, creativity, and innovation is created by the sneaking around trying not to be found out, and most importantly, people get to know each other better.

At the next team meeting everyone tries to guess who their secret squirrel was.

Friday shout

Just to celebrate the end of the working week (or make it hump day shout and do it on a Wednesday) the team can take turns at baking for or treating each other with a special weekly morning tea ritual.

Make a group mosaic or collage

Create a masterpiece together for your centre environment. This can be useful as group dynamics alter when there is a creative process at work (i.e. quieter people come out of their shells and extroverts need to concentrate more on the creative process so often talk less when their hands are busy). Creating something for the environment cements everyone's sense of belonging to the place when each day they see the product of their team building efforts.

Yoga/relaxation/massage/meditation/zentangle

Enlist the help of an instructor to teach the group or make a regular night and take turns at sharing your talents and passions.

External speakers

Get a motivational speaker in to teach your team a new skill like juggling, storytelling, learning ukulele, paper making – anything goes!

Spring clean your centre or spruce up the garden

Make sure there are plenty of opportunities for fun and rewards along the way.

Treasure hunts/scavenger hunts/car rally

Set a series of clues/riddles for teachers to solve as they learn more about each other and the environment and/or regulations.

Dress up parties

Always push people slightly outside their comfort zone which loosens them up for good social interaction (just add beer and wine).

Your team might enjoy meeting for special occasions out of work time, planning regular social meeting times, places, and events. Each team will be different and therefore will suit different activities. It is the leader's responsibility to ensure there is innovation, enjoyment, and purpose to the chosen activities.

You won't always get buy-in from everyone for each activity but if you continue to make them enjoyable, varied, and fun, even the staunchest of anti-social team members will eventually come around.

PHILOSOPHY IS THE STARTING POINT WHEN DEVELOPING A STRONG TEAM CULTURE

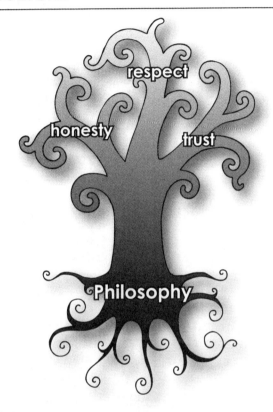

In this illustration I think of respect, honesty, and trust as being the fruits the tree is able to produce, but only when the philosophy is deeply embedded in the roots. It is the philosophy that is the vision and until everyone is on the same page with the philosophy and shared vision then the team can never get to the fruits of honesty, respect, and trust.

For example:

Sarah wants children to have only free play and Vanessa believes in structured environments and timetables for children. Forever more when Sarah throws open the doors and says "be free" a little part of Vanessa is angrily growling inside. Every time Vanessa rings her little bell and says "come in for mat time" Sarah is rolling her eyes. Until we all sit down and talk through the issues, philosophy, and vision, then we will have trouble with both camaraderie within the team and communication.

By beginning with a philosophy and shared vision we can create a culture of motivation, empathy and respect. This will most likely involve some team professional development and compromise between individual philosophies to reach a group consensus for the shared vision. We then need to continually revisit the vision as a team, ensure commitment from the whole team, make time to get to know each other outside of work, and deal with conflict openly and honestly.

HEALTHY TEAMS ARGUE SOMETIMES

In a healthy team, members work through issues with open discussion, lively debate, honesty, trust and respect. These things establish a loyalty within the team and each team member can feel strongly about a unified vision. The danger of peacefully co-existing where there is never any conflict, challenge or debate is that team members can become complacent and the vision and direction for the centre can be in danger of stagnation.

PLAN SUCCESSIONS AND PROMOTE FROM WITHIN

Part of the art of leadership is to spot a problem and solve it before it even arises. Leaders often find this skill to be an intuitive or "gut" feeling. I think it is more a case of assuming that everyone is moving on eventually so we should have a plan for this at all times. For example, if a manager gave notice tomorrow, do we know who would step up into their position? If a senior teacher becomes pregnant, do we have a replacement or temporary promotion in mind for maternity leave? Part of the art of leadership is having this giant jig-saw in our heads at all times that holds the myriad contingencies required should we lose any one part of the puzzle.

At Childspace we've always had a policy of promoting from within because it is our belief that the culture is one of the most crucial and defining factors of our success which sets us apart from other centres. When someone has been immersed in the culture, they are better able to share that and therefore inspire and lead others, than someone who has come from outside our organisation. This has meant that some, more experienced teachers and leaders, have had to accept a teaching position in order to establish their credibility within our organisation. It has also meant we've never been disappointed by hiring someone in a management position whose knowledge, attitude, and skills we were not absolutely certain about.

LEAVE A LEGACY

Over the years we have been fortunate to work with some truly amazing people. When they have moved on it has meant change for our organisation. Always they go with our blessing to continue their journey and touch the lives of others for the better. We accept that they have given what they can to our organisation and it is their time to move on. Rather than being devastated at not having their input any longer we feel fortunate for their service while they were with us. Our organisation will not be weaker because they are moving on; we will always be stronger because of the time, commitment and service they gave.

A way we have found to promote loyalty within our team of managers is to allocate a profit share at the end of each financial year. Of course this doesn't work on the rare occasions that our organisation doesn't make a profit for the year. The idea of a profit share gives us an opportunity to recognise and reward those managers in our organisation who have contributed and worked hard to ensure their enrolments are kept up and their teams are productive and happy.

Because it is in addition to the manager's salary it is a pleasant bonus for the manager when it happens. For our organisation this is a sustainable way to allocate a bonus because, rather than a raise in pay, which will be an ongoing additional expense, the bonus is not paid, or is reduced accordingly when times are tough financially.

SIMPLE SUMMATIVE ADVICE

People will only stay in a job they enjoy, so the most important aspect of fostering loyalty is to ensure each individual in your team enjoys their work and their colleagues. This will require opportunities to bond as a team and to work on collaboration to ensure a shared vision, philosophy, and goals. Recognise that healthy teams need to debate issues to ensure a greater understanding of shared vision. People come and go all the time from early childhood centre environments and it is important that we can accept these changes, plan for them by having great succession arrangements, and ensure loyalty is rewarded by promotion from within the team.

Be honest

" *Character makes trust possible. And trust makes leadership possible. That is the law of Solid Ground.* "

~John Maxwell

Chapter 6:

Be honest

Honesty means always directing any comments to the person concerned and encouraging all others to maintain the same high standard of communication with integrity. While we can also be tactful when being honest, we need to recognise that we are not responsible for how someone else reacts to our feedback. We have to admit when we've made a mistake, value and encourage feedback from others, and be reliable, predictable and the best version of our real selves.

Honesty is telling the truth even when this means we need to summon our courage and tact. We are honest when we are fair, truthful, sincere and frank.

"Honesty and integrity are absolutely essential for success in life - all areas of life. The really good news is that anyone can develop both honesty and integrity."

~ Zig Ziglar

Honestly, there is nothing else to be said about communication except for honesty. I am asked all the time "What would you do if....?" "How would you deal with......?" My answer every time is that I would be completely honest. No one can ask for anything more from me.

SPEAK DIRECTLY WITH THE PERSON CONCERNED

To set a culture of honesty and trust we need to model our ability to speak directly with the person concerned in the first instance consistently and without exception. We can also make it crystal clear to others within the team that it is our expectation for all team members. There are techniques in other chapters (team contracts and the DESC model) that can support us in having the courage to give direct feedback and be completely honest.

WE ARE NOT RESPONSIBLE FOR OTHERS' REACTIONS

Of course there is always a way to be honest while also being tactful so that we can avoid hurting the feelings of another person as much as possible. However, when it is necessary to give feedback that the listener doesn't want to hear, they may have negative emotional reactions such as anger or tears. This behaviour (much like a toddler) is meant to stop us from giving further feedback. It is important to recognise that we are not responsible for someone else's reaction to our honest and tactful (as possible) feedback. We can acknowledge their feelings while also establishing the need for them to listen and act on our feedback.

When feedback is objective, fact-based and not merely judgmental, people are less likely to take offence – however they still can and will confuse professional feedback with personal criticism. The only answer is to practice this skill so you can enable people to feel positively about feedback and not feel constantly on the defensive.

When we are working with children we know that in order to change behaviour without negatively affecting the self-esteem of the child, we must separate the behaviour from the child. This is also true when changing the behavior of adults. People can hear that a certain behaviour is unacceptable but it is judgmental and hurtful to be told that *they* are unacceptable.

WE NEED TO APOLOGISE WHEN WE ARE IN THE WRONG

Another essential element of honesty is admitting when we've made a mistake. Experience helps to shape our leadership so we learn from mistakes and should go easy on ourselves; we should accept these as part of our learning journey. We help to model and create an environment of honesty when we can admit that we have mucked up too, and then make a humble and sincere apology. What's more, team members find it refreshing to know that their leader is also human, and therefore makes mistakes just like everyone else.

BE AN AUTHENTIC LEADER

Honesty is being real. We should be exactly who we are (the best version of ourselves) because we will attract like-minded people who will pull together with common goals, philosophy and vision. Honesty will lead to trust and respect. Our team has to respect us before they will respect our ideas.

People soon appreciate that their leader is 100% honest without exception, and this will form the basis of trust within our working relationships. They will be more inclined to share information and seek advice when they can trust in our consistent honesty.

Honesty means being reliable and predictable. Good leaders are predictable in a productive way. When people come to us with feedback or for advice, they should be assured that we will have a predictable and positive first response. If we are always negative about feedback by interrupting, ignoring, or always having an excuse, thereby dismissing the feedback, we put people off bringing us feedback. We cannot improve without feedback, so we need to reframe how we feel about it. Rather than considering feedback a personal attack, consider it as a professional suggestion.

TRUST YOUR INTUITION

Problem solving is a natural tendency for great leaders. Thin-slicing is a term used in psychology and philosophy to describe the ability to find patterns in events based only on 'thin slices,' or narrow windows of experience. Many of us have learned to trust this thin-slicing as our gut instinct. Issues will often arise that require clarity of thought and calm problem solving. Such problem solving becomes automatic to a leader who is constantly aware of issues and experienced in handling situations to ensure the best possible outcomes for all stakeholders.

"Whenever leaders find themselves facing a problem, they automatically measure it – and begin solving it – using the Law of Intuition."
~John Maxwell

ASK YOURSELF A FEW HARD QUESTIONS

When we can be honest with ourselves about our own strengths and weaknesses, then we can make necessary improvements. Only with great courage and honesty can we address our own weaknesses.

The following are some interesting and courageous questions to ask yourself...

Why would somebody want to work with me?

Would I apply for a job to work with me?

What do I find most challenging about my job?

What steps could I take to improve my performance in that area?

Am I always addressing conflict and delivering feedback in a timely manner?

How could I make improvements to communication, conflict, and feedback?

Once upon a time I stumbled on a novel approach to feedback....

I had a team member who became quite emotional every time she was given even the slightest constructive criticism. Ironically, she was highly regarded for her peaceful approach with young children! But whenever someone gave her feedback there was an angry and negative reaction that would instinctively either make an excuse, blame someone else, or dismiss any idea or allegation out of hand.

Between us, we eventually figured out that when I was to give her feedback I would warn her it was coming and she literally held her hand over her mouth so she would listen to the feedback without immediately reacting. This technique worked for us because she was able to refrain from reacting and really listen and think about the feedback before reacting. Coupled with the opening statement each time "This is not personal and I want you to listen before reacting, please" we were able to negotiate a way to give and receive feedback peacefully.

SIMPLE SUMMATIVE ADVICE

Honesty is the simplest idea and yet it is one which many have difficulty with because being honest is not always easy and sometimes it is awkward. However, being an authentic leader requires honesty and team members will very quickly feel they can trust the integrity of an honest leader. Honesty means being reliable and predictable, apologising when we are in the wrong, always speaking directly with the person concerned, and honestly examining and working on our own areas of weakness.

Display grace

"Vision + Belief in everyone's' abilities and talents + Motivation for a common goal + Ensuring intrinsic satisfaction through meaningful engagement + Dash of grace = LEADERSHIP."

~ Karen Stephens

Chapter 7:

Display grace

When we display grace we are able to inspire confidence in our team through capable and calm decision making when faced with difficult situations. We use our power to create equality within a team so each member feels important and has a voice. We keep up to date with our learning and make conscious decisions to empower others through peaceful and courteous interactions even when faced with seemingly insurmountable problems.

Grace is having the moral strength to rise above difficult situations and disagreeable actions of other people. We show grace by maintaining a dignified demeanour in the face of adversity.

"*The ideal* [wo]man bears the accidents of *life with dignity* and *grace, making the best of circumstances*." – Aristotle

When I say display grace I don't mean like a ballet dancer. I mean that there is no situation we cannot rise above, and the true test of a leader is their ability to display grace in the face of adversity.

GRACE UNDER PRESSURE

When things happen that you never dreamed of in your life, you have to look as though you planned them... You have to have some sort of slight aura about you which is reassuring." ~ David Lange

Even when problems are difficult to solve, as so many are, we must present ourselves to our team gracefully, as being capable and in control. This might not be how we're feeling, but showing our anxieties or stress to others will only add to their own insecurities, and detract from our image as an unshakeable, confident, and competent leader.

When team members come to their leader with a seemingly insurmountable issue and their energy is anxious and worried, what they need is calm reassurance that we've got it under control. The last thing they need is for us to join in the panic and further exacerbate the situation.

A LEADER IS AN OPTIMIST

Similarly, when faced with an issue about which we have no choice – like the resignation of a key team member or a new regulation with which we must comply – there is absolutely no point in complaining about the situation. Graceful leadership means calmly and quickly measuring the problem, solving it, and presenting the solution in such a way that we all came up with a solution together.

THE GENTLE USE OF POWER

Power used wisely can create harmonious and synergistic teams. Leaders who are graceful in their use of power are respected within their teams, and have no reason to remind people that they hold the power. Leaders who misuse their power are often resented by the people in their teams; this can lead to challenges of authority and decisions which in turn leads to the insecure leader feeling the necessity to remind team members that they hold the power.

"Being in power is like being a lady. If you have to tell people you are, you aren't."
~ Margaret Thatcher

73

At all times we need to model an attitude that reinforces the fact that every person within the team is accountable for decisions and open to feedback. Therefore the answer is never "because I said so." The answer will be relayed with grace and patience to ensure relationships are respectful and all team members are on board with the big picture.

WE MUST MAKE PEACE WITH THAT WHICH WE CANNOT CONTROL

We are not responsible for what happens to us; we are responsible for how we respond to what happens, and we get to make that choice. For example it is easy to complain about the actions of another person or the life situation in which we find ourselves. However, this attitude will only make us and those around us feel worse. When we display grace, we choose to rise above the negativity and make a conscious decision to project positivity, calm, and peace.

Life has a way of throwing us seemingly insurmountable problems, situations, grief and chaos at any given time and our ability to endure and recover relies on our courage and grace. We don't dwell on setbacks or challenges in our personal or professional lives. Remember Eeyore from Winnie the Pooh? With his negative attitude and constant complaining, his character illustrates the qualities we've seen in some people we know. Ask yourself this: Are these people successful? Happy? Motivated? And which came first, all their bad news or the attitude that found bad news so easy to stick to?

"The ultimate measure of a person is not where he stands in moments of comfort and convenience, but where he stands at times of challenge and controversy."

~ Dr. Martin Luther King Jr.

OH LORD, IT'S HARD TO BE HUMBLE

Humility is the quality of having a modest and unpretentious view of our importance, ideas and abilities. When we are humble we are able to accept others ideas and recognise the good qualities and deeds of other people. We display grace when we are humble in our approach, and empower others by believing in and celebrating their unique strengths and talents.

"Leaders walk alongside us inspiring us to be more than who we think we are." ~ Pennie Brownlee

We display grace when we acknowledge that we are life-long learners and that, even though we are in a position of leadership, we must continually be learning and updating our knowledge to ensure we are leading our team with vision and passion.

"Leadership and learning are indispensable to each other." ~ JFK

In my travels as a keynote speaker at conferences, I am constantly surprised when other speakers only attend their own sessions. What do they hope to learn by listening only to themselves? And if they are still preparing their session then they need to take heed of the 7 P's discussed in this book!

I greatly admire Dr. Anne Meade, Karen Stephens, and others whom I have hosted as speakers at Childspace conferences. These people are the ones who attend the opening, closing, and every session in between.

It sometimes freaks me out when they attend my sessions but I greatly admire the fact that they are graceful enough to acknowledge that they are life-long learners and have much to be gained from listening to the ideas of others.

SIMPLE SUMMATIVE ADVICE

To lead with grace we must be humble enough to accept that we will always have much to learn. Optimism and acceptance are graceful qualities which will demonstrate to others that we can rise above difficult situations to create the best possible scenario for everyone involved. Our graceful reaction to situations will ensure that team members feel calm in our presence, and assured of our strength, courage, and wisdom.

Encourage creativity

" *Leadership is the ability to point your team in the same direction and reach your destination by delegating to their strengths.* "

~Vida Schurr

Chapter 8:

Encourage creativity

Encouraging creativity requires a huge amount of trust in those around us. So much trust that we can easily delegate to the strengths of others and feel comfortable that this will yield excellent results for the organisation. When we encourage creativity, we recognise the abilities of others, we resist the impulse to micromanage, we accept that others will do things differently than we would, and we admit that it is OK and often a desirable outcome!

Creativity is the ability to transcend traditional ideas, rules, patterns, and ways of being. When we are creative we can develop meaningful new ideas, forms, methods and interpretations. Creativity is risking what is for what could be.

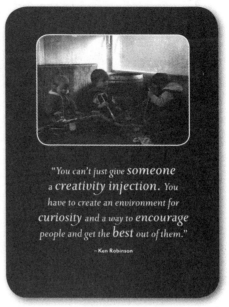

"You can't just give someone a creativity injection. You have to create an environment for curiosity and a way to encourage people and get the best out of them."

– Ken Robinson

An organisation will stand or fall on its ability to innovate and be continuously creative. Over the years our institute has been in business we have seen massive swings in funding and the entire removal of the provisionally registered teacher fund, which centres were often using as a general pool to fund professional development. We were creative about how, where, and when we could provide professional development that would cater to the ever-changing needs and funds of the sector.

WE ALL THINK AND DO THINGS DIFFERENTLY – AND THAT'S A GOOD THING

When we encourage creativity, we are open to the idea of others leading and doing things differently to how we might have done them. We can help people to think creatively by suggesting we don't want them to come to us with problems, but rather they should come with solutions whenever possible. To encourage creativity we really have to let go of our need to control everything. We also allow autonomy and initiative to thrive. When we have been given a task and the absolute freedom to execute it our own way, we will be far more likely to think outside the square, invest greater energy and hard-work to the task, and gain greater enjoyment of the process.

TRUST IN OTHERS' ABILITIES AND TALENTS

We have had two graphic designers in all the years we have been in business at Childspace, and these amazing women have been charged with creating everything from business cards, prospectuses, music CD artwork, magazines, calendars, catalogues, books, and much more. Our first graphic designer was part of a design company, and our current designer works at our home office, and is on the payroll like the rest of our team. Both designers would agree that I allowed them almost complete autonomy and encouraged their creativity when it comes to design work. Why? Because I am not a graphic designer! When we know our strengths and can appreciate and trust the strengths of those around us, then we encourage creativity because that is what will motivate others and inspire the best results.

IS THERE UNIFORMITY TO CREATIVITY?

Absolutely not! I'm aware that other opinions differ to mine on the subject of uniforms, but I have nothing good to say about uniforms at all. We're quite proud of the fact that both of our children have gone through the entire education system without having worn a uniform, and fundamentally I don't see the point in individual human beings dressing to look the same, unless for celebratory reasons that will give people a laugh. I always see a point in that sort of thing. We've had various tee shirts and sweat shirts printed over the years at Childspace for our team, but wearing them has always been an option.

Each of our centres is guided by an over-arching philosophy that every child is unique and requires acceptance and respect in order to develop to his or her full potential. While all the centres share this over-arching philosophy, they differ as to how this philosophy is embedded in practice, and how things look and feel. For example, one centre is enthusiastic about sustainability and environmental education, another is all about community engagement, one is focused very much on providing a home-like environment, and another is driven by the ideals of the Pikler approach. Each of these centres has evolved over time and, in accordance with the ideas, beliefs, and creativity of the team at each site, each setting has strengthened and added to that core philosophy in its own unique way.

Because we don't work with any one particular centre, we rely on the creativity of each team to drive their vision forward for the benefit of children and families. We encourage their creativity to grow and evolve, because it empowers the team to feel ownership of their philosophy and strengthens their beliefs and vision for children and families.

DELEGATION IS THE KEY TO UNLOCKING CREATIVITY

Great leaders aren't satisfied with simply getting others to follow them. Great leaders, in fact, lead other leaders.

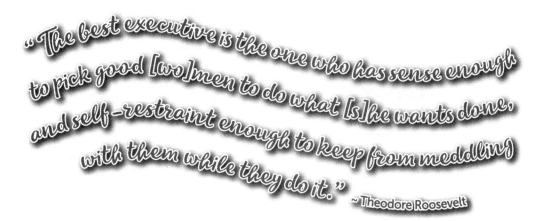

"The best executive is the one who has sense enough to pick good [wo]men to do what [s]he wants done, and self-restraint enough to keep from meddling with them while they do it." ~Theodore Roosevelt

People feel empowered when their leader delegates tasks. They feel this way because they are allowed to complete the task in their own way and time, thus encouraging creativity, and also because the leader they admire trusts them enough to allow them autonomy in executing the task. It is a very foolish leader who then watches over the execution of the task too much as they will have disempowered the person they wished to empower. Such micro-management often leads to resentful or discouraged staff. Leaders who micro-manage also create more work for themselves, when the point of delegation is to do the opposite.

When we delegate to a member of the team we need to use plenty of praise and highlight why we have chosen that team member. They need to feel flattered and not simply burdened with another task. Then it is a matter of giving the scope, timeframe, and the budget, if necessary, and then getting out of the way. We should always let those to whom we delegate know they can come back to us with questions or for feedback along the way. They should not have any doubt that we'd rather have queries throughout the process than failure as an end result.

I always ask for things at least a week before I need them. Whether I am giving a deadline for large construction work or a date for appraisal feedback forms to be returned, I give a deadline well in advance of when I will actually need it. This is my own simple safeguard so that I can accept with grace when someone fails to meet the deadline, give an extension, if needed, and not feel overwhelmed that the lack of timeliness might derail the whole vision, process, or project.

Like everything with leadership and management, sometimes we don't get the desired result we hoped for. The most important thing about failure is that we are resilient enough to pick ourselves up and try again, and that we learn from our mistakes. When delegating this might mean that the next time we choose a different person, give better directions, check in a little more often, or modify the task so it is better suited to the person.

While people have differing levels of creativity and express their creativity in different ways, I am convinced that we are all creative – we just have to tap into the most suitable form of creativity for each of our team members. For some, executing an entire production is the level that will challenge and inspire. For others, it might be a simple display board. It might be that one teacher can think creatively when faced with a problem that needs solving, but for another teacher, creativity means writing the parent newsletter. Through trial and error we can harness the collective strength and energy that surrounds us by encouraging creativity.

One of our centre managers is the absolute queen of delegation. I am constantly impressed by her ability to motivate and inspire others toward a common vision or goal. She appoints "ministers in charge of..." For example at her centre there is a minister in charge of first aid who ensures all the supplies and equipment are up to date and each teacher's practising certificate is renewed within the required timeframe. She appoints a minister in charge of stationery, arts and craft, self-review, engaging with community and so on.

This inspirational leader believes the idea of having ministers in charge has created a fun and playful way for members of her team to take on additional responsibilities. She believes the most important points regarding delegation are as follows:

Delegation must always be to the strengths of the individual. For example, there is a minister in charge of drawing plans for the environment who used to be a graphic designer.

The person to whom she delegates has to want the responsibility – they have to be motivated by the idea.

Both parties have to be fairly certain that the delegated role or task can be achieved by the person to whom it is delegated. Furthermore, if it is not, the delegator has to be willing to demote her minister.

Finally, this leader believes the key to her success is in trusting her team members and allowing them autonomy and creativity as to how their role or task is fulfilled.

SIMPLE SUMMATIVE ADVICE

Encouraging creativity is one way to ensure innovation in your early childhood setting. People are empowered to unlock their creativity when they are delegated tasks and given freedom to think outside the box. When we trust in other people's ability, and accept that they might think and act differently to us, we encourage them to think and act creatively. We are all creative on some level, and encouraging the unique creative talents of your team is an important part of leading with heart and soul.

Create joy

"Whenever you are creating beauty around you, you are restoring your own soul."

~ Alice Walker

Chapter 9:

Create joy

Teambuilding is essential to create trust, respect and joy within our environments. Getting to know our team members personally does not endanger our ability to act professionally but rather enables us to better understand and care for each other. When a leader has an enthusiastic and playful manner, their energy will be infectious and spread to create a joyful environment. Paying careful attention to the aesthetic in our environment helps us to create joy for all who enter our space and the act of creating joy for others delivers joy for ourselves.

Joy is the emotion of great delight and happiness caused by something exceptionally good or satisfying. We express joy when we exhibit keen pleasure and elation using both verbal and non-verbal language.

"Sometimes *your joy* is the source *of your* smile, but sometimes *your smile* can be the source of *your joy.*" —Thich Nhat Hanh

I'm the first to admit that if it's not fun, I'm not interested. Life is too short for workplaces to lack fun energy. So we need to think about the little ways we can inject joy into every day of our working lives, as well as the big plans we can make to create and maintain a joyful workplace.

SMILE AND LAUGH

Anyone who has worked in an environment where the leader lacks joy will attest how that creates a soulless place of work, devoid of joy. I once heard a saying that "a fish stinks from the head down," meaning that the head of the organisation sets the climate and culture. So if you walk into a place where there is unhappiness you will most often find an unhappy leader at the top. Simply smiling and laughing more often will create more joy in our lives and make us more open to possibilities and more likely to say yes to interesting adventures! Certainly smiles and laughter will reduce anxiety, stress and fatigue, so we should take every opportunity to create this joy in our lives.

Be miserable or motivate yourself. Whatever has to be done, it is always your choice. ~Wayne Dyer

ENTHUSIASM AND PLAYFULNESS

When we watch sporting teams we see them congratulate each other with high-fives, hugs, and celebrations in recognition of a good play. It is the same in our teams. We need to celebrate our achievements with smiles, laughter, hugs, high-fives and chocolate! All of these help to create a joyful and playful atmosphere.

We must also make time to celebrate our successes as a team. Perhaps we had a great review from our licensing authority, or a team member has a significant personal milestone. Taking time to mark these occasions with various forms of celebration will create joy for our workplaces and people.

SHOULD WE MIX OUR PERSONAL AND PROFESSIONAL LIVES?

One of the most obvious links to being able to create joy for our team is simply to share a personal bond with each individual. The idea that personal and professional lives should never mix is outdated and is also responsible for joyless workplaces where people feel disconnected. In early childhood our philosophy centres on the importance of relationships. This should be modelled throughout the organisation.

We also need to recognise that we walk a fine line between being supportive of teachers' personal lives and becoming an unpaid counsellor, or worse, a busy-body. There are boundaries and our own values and instincts will dictate when clarity is needed around those boundaries for the benefit of healthy team dynamics and relationships.

Sharing personal bonds and knowing each other well means we will more readily understand how and when we can support each other, and what our connection means as a model for our relationship-based curriculum. When there is genuine camaraderie in a workplace, then the team is able to function with greater synergy.

Some argue that keeping personal and professional lives separate is necessary because if we are too close to someone we might find it difficult to deliver appropriate, timely, and professional feedback. But if we are courageous and we have developed trust and respect within the team, then we will know someone better and be able to give more authentic feedback. We might go more gently and take care to differentiate that the feedback is professional and not personal. And we must always keep our words soft and sweet in case we have to eat them later.

"A sense of humour is part of the art of leadership, of getting along with people, of getting things done."
~ Harry S. Truman

TUNE IN OR TUNE OUT?

We can create more joy in our lives when we consciously limit the amount of negative news we expose ourselves to. Instead of turning on the news first thing in the morning, we can choose to exercise, meditate, walk, stretch, day-dream, and indulge in any number of other joyful and relaxing pursuits. The same can be said for the evening news. We can also tune out from the grumpy disposition of others by choosing not to engage with them. If they are a colleague we supervise, though, we must help them understand how their negative attitude impacts others.

SURROUND YOURSELF WITH BEAUTY

We should not underestimate the power of aesthetic to bring peace and joy to the soul. Just as children are more engaged in their play in a beautiful and orderly environment, we are more productive in our work when we surround ourselves with beauty and a sense of peace and calm. Fresh flowers, a beautiful table cloth, artwork on the walls, aesthetic displays and so much more, go into the creation of a beautiful staff room, office space, and early childhood classroom environment. When we take this sort of care with our surroundings we create joy for all who enter our space.

We create joy for others through generosity but the act of giving also creates joy for ourselves. At the end of each year at Childspace we have a prize giving event for our team. We all get dressed up, go out somewhere fancy, have dinner and drinks, listen to live music, and we hand out prizes. Lots of prizes! We give prizes for everything from excellence in learning stories to the most "out there" person in the team. We have silly prizes and serious prizes. This is an occasion that gives us the opportunity to let our team know that they are an incredibly special group of people who are hugely important in the lives of children and families.

This annual event brings joy to us all as we affirm individuals for their passion, commitment, and hard work throughout the year. It gives the message that we see and appreciate everything you do for the benefit of children.

SIMPLE SUMMATIVE ADVICE

Smile and laugh! Act in enthusiastic and playful ways. Don't be scared to establish and maintain personal bonds with team members. Reduce your dose of negative news and surround yourself with beauty.

Show gratitude

Success is glorious! When we recognise this we can celebrate the people around us and acknowledge their success; there are different ways to do this and all have the same message... 'We see and appreciate what you do'.

Chapter 10:

Show gratitude

Showing gratitude to others can be as simple as a smile and a "thank-you." In the general course of our busy work lives it can be easy to forget how necessary this courtesy is to the well-being, motivation, and sense of belonging of each member of a team. Showing gratitude to ourselves means we are kind to ourselves and conscious of the power of our negative and positive thoughts.

Gratitude is being thankful for who we are and what we have. We show our gratitude by thanking others through words and deeds and being kind to ourselves.

"One looks back with appreciation to the brilliant teachers, but with gratitude to those who touched our human feelings. The curriculum is so much necessary raw material, but warmth is the vital element for the growing plant and for the soul of the child." – Carl Jung

RECOGNITION MOTIVATES AND REWARDS

Nobody has so much intrinsic motivation that they will persevere with a difficult and demanding task if no one else recognises their effort. The social context of learning is such that we all need to be told how great we are a number of times before we believe it to be true. In fact, according to Dr. Rick Hanson, our brains have a hard-wired negativity bias. For example, we can be given ample positive feedback and yet the one negative comment will be the one that sticks with us, and the one that replays in our mind.

For this reason we need to deliver much more encouragement and positive reinforcement to every person in our team than constructive criticism. Hanson suggests that a healthy long-term relationship requires around a 5:1 ratio of positive to negative feedback. This means we need to be delivering five times more encouraging and positive feedback than constructive or negative feedback. However, it is important to note that children and adults alike are able to differentiate between praise that is appropriate and praise that is meaningless.

HOW IS CONSTRUCTIVE CRITICISM DIFFERENT TO CRITICISM?

We also need to understand the difference between constructive criticism and mere negativity.

When we communicate constructively we...

- Acknowledge strengths first.

- Separate the individual from his or her behaviour.

- Reinforce the supportive nature of our workplace – that the person will have support in making any required changes.

- Ensure everyone understands what is expected.

- Express confidence in the person's ability to meet our needs.

- Check in, follow up, and ensure everyone knows they can seek further advice or clarification as they move forward with suggestions.

WHAT MOTIVATES EACH INDIVIDUAL?

Leaders must know their people. We must know what drives each individual. For example people react differently to praise; for some it is essential and for others it is embarrassing. For some people pay is a strong motivating factor; for others, greater responsibility or recognition is more valued. There are also different methods of delivery which suit different individuals at different times. It is a leader's challenge to know what methods and types of motivation best suit each teacher. When we show a generosity of spirit then praise and gratitude come easily, and the people around us are motivated by our genuine and generous gratitude.

"Feeling gratitude and not expressing it is like wrapping a present and not giving it."
~ William Arthur Ward

IT'S NOT ABOUT THE MONEY

Generosity is not all about money. Because we are always working to a strict budget in order to make our organisations financially viable we need to be clever about ways we can show gratitude that don't cost a cent. For example:

- Smile and say "thank-you."
- Offer your time and make time for the person to whom you are grateful.
- Give a bouquet of flowers from the garden.
- Create a hand-made card or write a letter with beautiful words of gratitude.
- Provide public recognition like praise in front of parents or a mention in the newsletter.
- Gather thanks in writing from members of the team about each other and share at a staff meeting.
- Use a found object such as a feather or stone as a gift with some heart-felt words of gratitude.
- Pay full attention.
- Smile and make people laugh.
- Offer to help with something the person needs to do.
- Give a compliment.
- Make a playlist of music they like.
- Provide tickets to a concert.
- Have a scavenger hunt with fun clues.
- Provide lunch.
- Organise a clothing exchange where everyone brings what they no longer wear, so that everyone benefits from a new item of clothing.
- Create a photo album or make a frame for a great photo.
- Give an acrostic poem or other similar piece of creative poetry.

LIVE IN GRATITUDE

When we live in gratitude we consciously count the things for which we are thankful. Having an attitude of gratitude ensures our life is filled with positivity and love. There are many things that impact us that are outside of our control, however we can control our thoughts and our thoughts are incredibly powerful in determining our enjoyment of life.

Showing gratitude is not just about how we demonstrate generosity towards others but also how we treat ourselves and control our own negative thoughts and turn them into positive thoughts. This means thinking about what is good in our lives instead of what is bad, thinking about what we do have instead of what we don't, what we love instead of what we hate, who loves us instead of who doesn't, and so on. When we can be grateful for our own gifts and talents we find it easier to identify the gifts and talents of those around us.

Once upon a time one of my responsibilities as principal of our early learning centres was to deliver appraisals and feedback to our entire staff including our five centre managers. One ritual I started was to write a personal letter to each manager. This letter outlined the positive feedback identified through the appraisal process, as well as my own comments highlighting my gratitude for all their hard work and enthusiasm in their role as centre manager. The letter was a small token which created joy for both the receiver and me, the writer.

These days our principal writes these letters to her managers, and I know some of our managers have extended the ritual to include writing to each of their teachers at appraisal time. I now write a card for each of my team at home office (two administrators, two accountants, a graphic designer and the Childspace principal).

Here is an example:

Dear Memory,

Over the three years you have been principal at Childspace, you have grown in the role so much. Now you are going to literally grow while in the role for the last few months as you prepare to welcome your mini-mem into the world. We could not be happier for you and Reesh at this beautiful news. We will always consider you to be part of our family and we will always be grateful to you for the service, commitment and dedication you have given to your various roles at Childspace. You will leave a leadership legacy when you finish as principal and you have carefully selected your successor.

Thank-you

Here are some comments from your team who love you very much!

- *"Memory is a visionary."*

- *"It's actually amazing how one person can be so adept at everything she does. She's a little treasure."*

- *"She is an inspiring leader and mentor."*

- *"Memory makes us feel valued, appreciated and special."*

- *"She is an amazing advocate for respecting children and believes in the Childspace philosophy and way."*

- *"She creatively initiates new projects, ideas, and actions them."*

- *"Memory is grounded within herself and is extremely friendly, approachable, kind-hearted, and considerate."*

We have been truly honoured and blessed to have you in our organisation and look forward to welcoming your new arrival next year and staying in touch regarding coming back to work part time in the role of SELO co-ordinator.

SIMPLE SUMMATIVE ADVICE

Recognition motivates and rewards the people around us, as does a simple smile and "thank-you." Constructive criticism separates the person from their behaviour and is delivered in such a way that enables the receiver to feel acknowledged and supported to make improvements. People are not motivated purely by money, which is fortunate as ours is not a high-paying profession! When we live in gratitude, we fill our lives with positivity and love.

Empower others

" The role of leader is not to get other people to follow but to empower others to lead. "
~ Bill George.

Chapter 11:

Empower others

We can empower our team when we have effective appraisal systems in place that are well understood and user-friendly. We must actively work on succession plans to ensure if someone moves on we'll have a clear idea of how we might handle the transition with relative ease. We look for natural leaders in the organisation and promote them to ensure they have the opportunity to lead others in the same direction as the central vision, and not off down the garden path! A few useful tools for empowering others are the formulation of a team contract, the GROW model for mentoring, and the commitment to praise in public and criticise in private. We must give power to others to get the best from them. We all want to be appreciated, rewarded, capable, and successful. Leaders create the climate where this is possible because team members feel appreciated and respected and are therefore motivated.

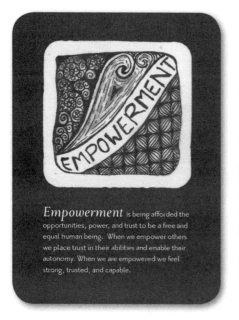

Empowerment is being afforded the opportunities, power, and trust to be a free and equal human being. When we empower others we place trust in their abilities and enable their autonomy. When we are empowered we feel strong, trusted, and capable.

"Education remains the key to both economic and political empowerment." – Barbara Jordan

GROW – A GREAT MODEL FOR MAKING IMPROVEMENTS

When mentoring, coaching, appraising, and thereby empowering members of our teams we use the GROW model for inspiration. The GROW model was originally developed in the 1980s by performance coach Sir John Whitmore, although other coaches, such as Alan Fine and Graham Alexander, have also helped to develop it, and there have since been many claims to authorship of the well-known and widely used model. I was first introduced to this technique through a post-graduate paper at Victoria University on coaching, mentoring and professional development. Since this time we have used the model for self-review, appraisal, coaching, mentoring, and conflict resolution at Childspace.

GROW

G Goal – *what do you want to happen?*

R Reality – *what is currently happening?*

O Options – *what are all the options for improvement?*

W Will – *what will you commit to?*

When systems for improvement are clear and simple we are far more likely to bring about improvements and empower participants to take ownership of the process.

APPRAISAL AND TEACHER REGISTRATION WORK TOGETHER TO IMPROVE TEACHER PRACTICES

Teacher registration in New Zealand is one of the main ways that employers, colleagues, learners and the wider community can be assured that a teacher is qualified and competent. Appraisal and teacher registration can be highly effective avenues for empowering the members of our team. We link the two together so that we are not doubling up on paperwork.

Each member of our team keeps a teaching story which is a record of all relevant exemplars of their teaching, teamwork and necessary evidence for teacher registration. This folder is collected by the centre manager twice annually and an appraisal interview is conducted based on the identified short and long-term goals and rewards for each individual. At these formal interviews we are able to identify necessary improvements or direction for teacher registration, as well as programme, curriculum, and teamwork, which is also very relevant to the criteria and key indicators for teacher registration.

> **Effective performance appraisal systems...**
> * promote reflection and quality improvements.
> * are simple, clear, and easy to use.
> * are open, honest, supportive, and friendly.
> * enable teachers to feel positive about themselves.
> * are ongoing and have both formal and informal components.
> * are collaborative.
> * are bottom-up as well as top-down.
> * provide opportunities for relationship-based understanding.
> * are relevant to other criteria such as teacher registration and/or job descriptions and professional development.
> * have goals and rewards.
> * recognise abilities and celebrate learning and improvements.
> * give direction and vision.
> * promote career development.
> * follow through on goals and rewards.

PRAISE IN PUBLIC, CRITICISE IN PRIVATE

One of the simplest strategies for empowering others is to ensure that any constructive advice or guidance is delivered directly and only to the person involved. It is essential that we create a public perception that there are no issues within the team. Privately, we can work out anything that needs to be addressed but publicly discussing issues only leads to a weakened perception of the strength of the team. This idea of praising in public and criticising in private also works for marriages and teenagers!

TEAM CONTRACTS EMPOWER US ALL

Something we have found useful at Childspace over the years is the idea of individual empowerment through the development and adherence to team contracts. Creating a team contract provides opportunities to share information about individual wants and needs in the work place, as well as helping to clarify expectations of professional behaviour.

To create a team contract we simply come together as a team and discuss what is important to us, ways in which we can all respectfully work together, and the minor details and practicalities as to how that might happen. The process allows us to learn and understand more about our colleagues and ensures everyone is clear about our vision, roles and expectations. It sets boundaries for collegial behaviour, and gives a common reference point when these boundaries are pushed. Because it is developed collaboratively and everyone has agreed to the conditions, adherence to the contract thereby creates a harmonious work environment.

Ngaio Childspace Team Treaty

Here at Ngaio Childspace we will commit to:

- *Sharing the love; smiles and salutations are part of the caring and respectful culture we have created.*

- *Through modelling respect, we strive to create a pedagogy of listening: to each other, to the children and to the families with whom we work.*

- *Be considerate: give praise where praise is due and approach differences of opinion with integrity and grace.*

- *Be clean.*

- *Share our strengths, praise each other's achievements and choose our mindsets.*

- *Reflect our philosophy in our teaching practice. Slow down, be gentle, and be aware of sound.*

- *Being flexible: following the cues and rhythms of children's needs and ideas. We will adjust adult time schedules in accordance with these needs.*

- *Keep the environment aesthetically inspiring and innovative. Flowers, candles, fabric and fun are the spice of life.*

- *Treasuring the relationships we build with families, maintaining professional and respectful bonds.*

- *Role model respecting our resources and handling them with care.*

- *Enjoy nature. Forage in the forests, recycle where possible and be kind to mother earth.*

- *Feed each other treats and be thankful for everyone's hard work.*

- *Be kind.*

Home office chicks rock the house!

- We always engage in open and honest communication and we discuss our concerns with the person they involve. Furthermore, we are assertive in directing others within our organisation to do the same.

- We encourage open communication by responding appropriately to constructive feedback.

- We care for our beautiful work environment by cleaning up after ourselves in the kitchen, ensuring our office spaces are tidy and presentable, not leaving mess in other offices or our main presentation spaces, and always locking up the building thoroughly.

- We respect each other's roles and responsibilities and take extra care not to overburden each other.

- We perform our own roles to the best of our ability and can be relied upon to meet expectations and deadlines in a timely manner. We focus on work at work.

- We promise to let each other know when we might need extra support for either professional or personal reasons.

- We are respectful that this is a shared workspace and allow each other to concentrate by generally using quiet voices to communicate – except when we are laughing so loud we pee our pants!

- We are a team and recognise the need to truly support each other – we are relying on each other to succeed and if one of us fails we all fail.

- We are able to relax and enjoy each others company outside of work as well as making our workplace a fun and enjoyable place to be.

- We endeavor to be environmentally friendly by composting, recycling, giving our kai scraps to Toni's pigs, looking after our garden & any other initiatives which promote sustainable practices.

- We promise to smile, laugh, have fun and share all the chocolate, lollies and love.

Childspace
Early Childhood Institute

45 Helston Road, Johnsonville,
Wellington 6037, New Zealand.
Phone: (+64 4) 461 7076 • Fax: (+64 4) 478 3986
Email: institute@childspace.co.nz

SUCCESSION PLANNING

Succession planning is all about empowering others and also ensuring the organisation remains strong when people move on. We need to constantly think about which members of our team are ready for the next challenge and actively prepare them to take their next step in their professional journey.

Plenty of early childhood centres have failed after years of service to the community when there was no succession plan in place. Life can be uncertain, so we don't know when we might have to step away from our position as leader either temporarily or permanently. We must ensure that we are not the only person who knows how to do things. If we are always working on succession planning then we can be comforted by the knowledge that someone is able and ready to step up in our absence. Given the stress involved in the kind of life-changing situations that might require us to leave our position, it is a comfort to know we have someone available who can fill our role.

" If your actions inspire others to dream more, learn more, do more, you are a leader. "

~ John Quincy Adams

NURTURE LEADERSHIP IN OTHERS

Embrace natural leaders. These are the people others look to and follow. You probably know plenty of people like this. They are the ones who are laughing and giggling and getting everyone else to laugh and giggle with them when you are trying to get focus from the team at a meeting. Get these natural leaders involved in the bigger picture. Promote them or delegate responsibilities that will continue to challenge them and hone their leadership capabilities.

I used to play netball before my knees got old. I also loved to coach and was a netball coach for fourteen years; I coached at all different levels from premier grades to beginners when my children started out in the sport.

One year I had a particularly spirited group of 15-year-old girls. I was only about 19 years old myself and playing at a much higher level. One particular girl in the team was giving me a lot of trouble. She had difficulty taking direction, but she also seemed to be very popular with the rest of the team; she would derail my training sessions, and lead the others in fooling around when I was attempting to get focus within the team.

My instinct told me that if I made this girl captain she could rise to the challenge and get on board with my direction and vision. Sure enough, this was exactly what happened. Upon becoming captain, this natural leader had instant focus, and because she already had influence within the team, this brought the other players into line. I was able to gain the focus of the team and to have productive training sessions and successful competition results.

Awfully proud of my 19 year old clever self, I told my own coach this story after one of our training sessions and she raised her eyebrows and said, "What a good idea, Toni."

It was not until after training that evening that I reflected how she had made me captain of her team too!

SIMPLE SUMMATIVE ADVICE

Empower natural leaders and get them on board with your vision and direction. Share your knowledge and have a plan for succession in each of your organisation's key roles. Develop a team contract with the team to help clarify expectations of professional behaviour. Ensure performance appraisal systems are simple, effective, and well-understood by everyone involved. Use a model like GROW to ensure you are constantly improving and empowering your team.

Model respect

" Success is liking yourself, liking what you do, and liking how you do it. "
~ Maya Angelou

Chapter 12:

Model respect

Respecting ourselves is the most important thing we can do as leaders. It is the secret to success in every other area of management and leadership. We model respect by trusting our intuition, accepting our mistakes as learning opportunities, and not taking other people's problems on board. Getting enough sleep and exercise is also a matter of self-respect, as is using our time efficiently, and ensuring our work life rocks! We can always make improvements through self-awareness and self-mentoring.

Respect is the key to relationships. When we show consideration for another person, we communicate to them that they are valued. Feeling valued contributes to a sense of trust and self-esteem and is reflected in the individual's ability to form and maintain relationships with others.

"A person's a person no matter how small."

– Dr. Seuss

This chapter is probably the most important for all leaders to understand and keep foremost in their mind if they seek longevity in their career. Without self-respect all the other values about leadership mean nothing, because we cannot be courageous, empower others, show gratitude, create joy, dream big, have empathy, foster loyalty, be honest, display grace, encourage creativity, or serve others without first respecting ourselves.

"I am my own experiment. I am my own work of art" ~ Madonna

Relaxation. A little relaxation goes a long way. We can build downtime into our schedules and protect our leisure time. It is important that some of this is solitary time.

Exercise. People complain "I don't have time to exercise" – I think none of us has time NOT to! It is counterintuitive but moderate exercise that is enjoyable actually increases our energy levels so we function better and can fit more into every day!

Sleep. Getting enough sleep is the key to high level functioning of the body, brain and all our organs. When we can get to bed early enough we can wake feeling refreshed. We also need to tell ourselves that we are good sleepers – the subconscious is so powerful that when we complain to ourselves or others that we cannot sleep – indeed we won't.

Play! Life is short. Play more!

Energy. We need to guard our energy and drop activities that sap our time or energy. It's OK to say "no" and that is exactly what we need to do to the friend who only gossips, the group we no longer enjoy, the committee going nowhere...

Create! Creativity is an incredible outlet for self-expression and imagination.

Time to relinquish some control, spread the responsibility, delegate and say "yes" to offers of help.

"Rest and self-care are so important. When you take the time to replenish your spirit, it allows you to serve others from the overflow. You cannot serve from an empty vessel."

~Eleanor Brownn

WORK LIFE ROCKS!

We hear a lot about "work-life balance" and certainly it is important to have balance in our lives, but I think the whole idea of work-life balance sets us up for failure and creates anxiety. For example we usually only hear people talk about work-life balance when indicating that they don't have it, and that they are striving to achieve it (and don't believe they'll ever get there). Basically, I think they just use the term as a crutch to suggest they are working too hard and not having enough time to themselves. While I agree with the concept that we need a balance in all things, I think I prefer the term "work-life rocks!"

Working hard for something we don't care about is called stress; working hard for something we love is called passion.

The first key to ensuring your work life rocks is to love your work! Next we must understand what balance actually means. If it is 5pm on a Friday and that is the time we are supposed to finish but we have another hour of work to do so we can be truly free to enjoy our weekend, then balance means we should do the extra hour so we can really enjoy the weekend off. Too often people are inclined to think work-life balance means they are supposed to finish at 5pm so that is when they'll finish, regardless. But they take home with them the worry, stress, and anxiety that the extra hour of work will be waiting for them on Monday morning and therefore can't enjoy their weekend as they should.

USE A DIARY FOR BETTER TIME MANAGEMENT

When we can use our diary or calendar effectively and prioritise tasks, we get the important tasks completed first. Then we can leave work and be fully present at home knowing our diary has all the important information stored for the next day. We don't have to spend the time we should be relaxing worrying about what needs to be done or remembered. We also need to ensure we have good and efficient systems in place to get things done when we are at work, and reward ourselves for good time management.

FURTHER TIPS FOR TIME MANAGEMENT

The tips below will take us a long way towards maximising our task-oriented time:

- Prioritise and delegate tasks. Do what is important first and delegate to the strengths of others in the team.
- Keep meetings short and focussed. When we have a clear agenda that has circulated prior to the meeting, we are able to get maximum results in minimum time. We also have to be focussed about chairing meetings, keeping them on task, and moving onto the next agenda item in a timely manner.
- Learn to say "no". We can soon overburden ourselves and end up doing lots of things to a less than acceptable standard if we are not self-aware enough to realise our own limits. It is far better for everyone if we only commit to what we know we can deliver to a high-quality standard, which will mean saying "no" occasionally.
- Read selectively and faster. Leaders read and readers lead so there will always be reading in a leadership role. However, we can be clever about what, when and how much we have to read in order to stay abreast of recent legislation, research and developments. We can start with the conclusion in some instances and let that dictate whether we are

interested or motivated to read back through the full report. We can keep a stack of reading for times when it is appropriate or able to be done. My stack, for example, is usually by my bed at home as there are too many interruptions at work. As with anything else, delegation can be used to great effect with reading. When we know something is of special interest to one of our team then we can ask them to read and report back.

- Strive to gain some time to day-dream.

- Avoid attending useless meetings. A useless meeting is one that takes your time and motivation without delivering any benefit to you or your organisation.

The paradox of caring for others is that it is both hugely rewarding AND stressful. The most important thing we can do is love ourselves. "People who love themselves come across as very loving, generous and kind. They express their self-confidence through humility, forgiveness and inclusiveness." ~ Sanaya Roman

THIS IS NOT MY CIRCUS – THESE ARE NOT MY MONKEYS

This phrase was coined by Onchen and Wass in 1974 in an article in the *Harvard Business Review*. It has since been used by dozens of other business gurus to explain how managers can avoid becoming walking lint collectors for their subordinates' problems.

When we find ourselves in a position of leadership, we will also find there are team members who consider it part of our role to take on their problems, issues, baggage and attitudes from time to time. When this happens we can think about the idea of monkeys. Each person carries with them, on their shoulder, their own monkey. The monkey is a metaphor for all that each person brings with them to their current context – their emotional baggage, attitudes and problems.

A good leader can feed, pat, and water another person's metaphorical monkey without actually taking it on board. In other words, we can give our full attention, offer advice, empathy, and compassion. But we must beware of taking the other person's monkey on board ourselves, as we already have our own monkey, and one is enough for each person as these beasts do not cohabitate.

So when we find ourselves being pulled into other people's drama, trying to solve other people's problems, or taking on board too much of another person's anxiety or issues, we must remember – not my circus; not my monkeys!

"When you're captain of your own ship and that ship sails in its not luck." ~ Patti Smith

BE KIND TO THE CAPTAIN

We need to go easy on ourselves. No one is perfect, and even though we strive for excellence we will never be perfect. We will make mistakes and we will sometimes get things wrong. It is crucial that we are kind to ourselves at these times and recognise that any failures are simply learning opportunities. We can reflect on how we might do things better next time, and move on without beating ourselves up about it.

BE A GREAT SELF-MENTOR

In one of her many brilliant early childhood leadership books, Paula Jorde Bloom identified some questions to get leaders started on self-mentoring, this disposition of lifelong learning and self-transformation. These are:

What is really important to you? What do you value most?

What special talents make you unique?

What qualities to do you most admire in others?

How do you define personal success? When have you felt most successful?

When have you felt most alive, energised, and excited about work? When have you felt most depleted and discouraged about work?

How do you think others see you?

How do you handle adversity? Are you quick to blame others when things don't go well or do you take ownership for the outcome of your decisions and actions?

When do you feel most at peace?

Have you achieved a reasonable sense of balance in your life between your personal and professional pursuits?

How do you regulate your emotions? Do you let emotions get in the way of interpersonal relationships?

Do you often compare yourself to others?

What do you want more of in your relationships and what do you want less of?

What legacy do you want to pass on?

Respect and empathy are intertwined; both are essential for sustaining vibrant and authentic relationships. When we show consideration for another person we communicate to them that they are valued. Feeling valued contributes to a sense of trust and self-esteem and is reflected in the individual's ability to form and maintain relationships with others.

Respect gives the message....

- I am listened to or not.
- What I choose to do is valued or it isn't.
- How I express my emotions is accepted or it isn't.
- I am allowed to explore or I am not.
- My needs are met or they are not. ~ Dr. Ronald Lally

Once upon a time....

I was just 21 years old when we opened Childspace. Throughout the years I feel I have learned so many lessons that have educated my heart and soul. I can honestly say that I look back at some of the decisions I've made, and things I have said and done, and I cringe! Had I known then what I know now, I'm certain I would have handled each situation with a great deal more grace, tact, compassion, respect, patience, kindness, humility, and gratitude.

Respecting myself means I haven't beaten myself up about these situations. I have been able to learn from the mistakes, grow in experience and knowledge, and ensure I handle things better next time. I am reassured by the idea that each of us can only do the best we can, with the information we have, at any given time.

SIMPLE SUMMATIVE ADVICE

When we can model respect for others we demonstrate self-love and self-care. There are many simple tips to improving our time management and working smarter, not harder. We must be kind to ourselves and beware of others' monkeys!

To conclude

Leadership requires great personal courage to be honest with ourselves and others – to be real, think creatively, trust our instincts and back our vision with hard work and enthusiasm. A team cannot make improvements, and offer the best possible outcomes for children and families, without communicating courageously to resolve conflict and differing perceptions.

Dreaming big is what distinguishes leadership from the more process-oriented tasks of management. It is not enough simply to dream big, but we must also have the ability to share our vision and create strategic plans with which the entire team is on board. Dreaming big is about making time for day-dreaming, striving for excellence, avoiding complacency, celebrating our achievements, employing initiative and planning effectively. Sharing vision promotes unity and loyalty within a team. We also foster loyalty by promoting from within, offering incentives, creating camaraderie and a strong team culture of honesty and respect.

Our generosity of spirit and willingness to serve others provides a model to our team, which creates empathy and respect within the working environment. This empathy will enable us to see from multiple perspectives, to listen, value, and meet the needs of our team members. We are then able to delegate to the strengths of those around us, and make the best decisions for the health of our organisation, and achieve the best outcomes for children and families.

Being honest ensures we are reliable, predictable and the best version of ourselves. It also provides a model for other members of our team and sets a culture of honest communication, which is integral to a healthy work culture. Displaying grace under pressure inspires confidence, clarity and calm within our team.

We encourage creativity and empower others when we can trust in the strengths and talents of everyone in the team. We readily delegate tasks and team members gain confidence in using their own initiative and creativity. This creates joy within the environment and an infectious energy of motivation. When a leader has an enthusiastic and playful manner, when there are opportunities for team members to trust, respect and care for each other, then joy will permeate the work environment.

Showing gratitude is essential for the healthy self-esteem of team members. It is motivational because we are more likely to repeat or improve on an action for which we have been given encouragement or praise. Showing gratitude to ourselves means we are kind to ourselves and conscious of the power of our negative and positive thoughts. Only when we respect ourselves can we respect others.

Leadership in early childhood is by no means child's play. Rather, it is extremely complex and requires highly motivated, empathetic, visionary, intelligent, and intuitive people. In this book I have shared some of my core values for leadership. Each chapter is only a brief outline and my hope is that this small offering may inspire and motivate readers to examine their own core values and be the best leader they can be, for the benefit of their colleagues, families, and the children in their lives.

Lead with heart and soul. Our children deserve no less.

Backword
From Karen Stephens

Oh yes, I know what you're thinking. This should be titled an "Afterword," not a "Backword."

But "Afterword" just sounds too conventional for a Christie book, much less for the Childspace approach to the world. My much-respected friend and admired colleague, Dr. Paula Jorde Bloom, wrote a fantastic Foreword, so it makes perfect sense that I write a Backword. To do so is to act in the perpetual playful way of the Christies. And so, I rest my case. (And anyway, I'm like our author Toni; I'm always more interested in doing something if there's a bit of fun in it.)

In this Backword, I encourage you to "go back" to Toni's words to fully absorb them. Play around with them to squeeze out every bit of wisdom and all the practical tips you can.

Here's how I go "back word" in a really good book. I revisit all the parts I highlighted with my ever-ready marker. (Surely, dear fellow reader, you had yours handy, too. If not, go back to brighten up select morsels! Color away, you have lots from which to choose!)

I review tidbits I underlined. And I re-visit the comments I penned into the margins—some of which support the text "Yea, right on!" and some of which challenge it, (Say what, Girlfriend?!)

I take time to ponder paragraphs I punctuated with a star, exclamation point, question mark, a smiley face or perhaps a growling frown. (A book read without leaving such punctuation marks is hardly a book read at all!) If your book isn't all marked up, go back and do the job properly. As any good educator knows, revisiting ideas is good brain science in action.

I like to share good books with my peer professionals. Reading the same book offers a team common ground for discussion and brainstorming. After all team members have read (and decorated) their book, have them trade books to explore others' margin comments. It's a great way to notice important ideas missed in an initial reading.

Another follow up activity is a team review in a book club format. For instance, go back to ponder Toni's distinction between leadership and management duties. Can team members estimate the ratio of time spent on leadership vs. management duties? Is the ratio working for them? If not, which of the book's ideas could be helpful?

Toni's writing does far more than just identify leadership characteristics. She also shares methods of motivating followers to collaborate for the greater good. Ask staff to search out those ideas in the book and reflect on them. Ponder ways your team collaborates well, or not? Through team planning, set goals for collaboration progress.

To dig even deeper into the book, ask staff to identify their favourite "take away" ideas. Which ideas are a good "match" for your staff and programme? Which could be implemented tomorrow, in a month, a quarter, in a year? Who needs to be involved? Who can take a leadership role in each step toward application? There is so much rich discussion awaiting you!

A primary way I judge a book is to reflect on whether or not the author made her point convincingly. In my estimation, yes, Toni Christie did! She convinced me that the clarity of our values and their consistent, creative application is important at every turn of our professional practice. Has she convinced you and your staff?

I detected Toni Christie's core message early in her introduction. Of working in early childhood she said, "If your heart and soul aren't in it, then neither should you be." Whoa. There's no tiptoeing around that opinion. She threw down the challenge in no uncertain terms: either jump into serving children and families giving it your complete best effort or please earn a living elsewhere. (Rather cheeky of her, I think. But also, spot on!)

I'm convinced that Toni's "heart and soul" approach is golden. To offer less is to short-change the quality of life on all of Planet Earth. Our daily programme practices either nurture children's optimal development or not. We either support families to be functional or we don't. Toni reminds us that there is a lot at stake when you interact with children and families, especially during their most vulnerable and formative stage of life: early childhood and family building.

Jim Greenman, a famed deep-thinker and early childhood programme innovator, often said that when serving children and families, staff must be the very best person we can be, NOT just the best professional we can be. In that vein, Toni's writing has convinced me that such service requires us to be clear on our values. And it requires us to lead with our whole heart and soul—no matter our job title. To do less is to let down those we cherish most: the tamariki, the children.

So I leave you to have a look at it. And in case you're curious, here's my favourite "take away" from the book: Make JOY a part of your heart and soul leadership process! (For a refresher on that point, please refer to section title, "The Team That Plays Together Stays Together.")

Thank you to Toni Christie for allowing me the privilege of sharing this little Backword. And especially, dear valued reader, THANK YOU for caring enough to read and to lead on behalf of children and families. You make all our lives better by your actions.

Till our paths cross,

Karen Stephens

Emeritus Director of Illinois State University Child Care Center and child development instructor in ISU Department Family and Consumer Sciences, Normal, Illinois, USA

References and further reading

Bloom, P. J. (2014). *Leadership in action: How effective directors get things done* (2nd ed.). Lake Forest, IL: New Horizons.

Bloom, P. J. (2007). *From the inside out: The power of reflection and self-awareness.* Lake Forest, IL: New Horizons.

Bower, S., & Bower, G. (2004). *Asserting yourself: A practical guide for positive change* (Revised ed.). Beverly, MA: Da Capo Press.

Claxton, G. (2002). *Building learning power.* Bristol, United Kingdom: Henleaze House.

Erikson, E. (1972). Early infancy. In Smart, R. C., & Smart, M. S. (Eds.), *Readings in child development and relationships* (pp. 27–30). New York: Macmillan.

Hanson, R. (2013). *Hardwiring happiness: The new brain science of contentment, calm, and confidence.* New York: Harmony Books.

Hubbard, A. (2003). David Lange on love, labour, loss. *Star Times,* April 20.

Katz, L., & McClellan, D. (1997). Principles of practice for enhancing social competence. In Fostering social competence. *The teacher's role.* (pp. 49–61). Washington: NAEYC.

Maxwell, J. (1998). *The 21 irrefutable laws of leadership.* Nashville, TN: Thomas Nelson.

Ministry of Education. (1996). *Te Whāriki early childhood curriculum.* Wellington, New Zealand: Learning Media.

Poole, J. (2011). *Leadership in easy steps.* Southam, United Kingdom: Easy Steps Limited.

Education Council. (2012). www.educationcouncil.org.nz/required/Registration_Policy

Rodd, J. (2013). *Leadership in early childhood The pathway to professionalism* (4th ed.). Sydney: Allen & Unwin.

Thornton, K., Wansborough, D., Clarkin-Phillips, J., Aitken, H., & Tamati, A. (2009). *Conceptualising leadership in early childhood education in Aotearoa New Zealand.* Occasional Paper No. 2. Wellington: New Zealand Teachers Council.

Appendix 1:
21 more values cards (12 used in chapters)

Beauty is the quality present in a thing or person that gives intense pleasure or deep satisfaction to the mind. When we are beautiful on the inside, that beauty radiates outwards. We teach aesthetic and care when we surround ourselves with beauty.

"The **human soul** needs actual **beauty** more than bread."
- D H Lawrence

Generosity is sharing what we have and who we are with others. When we are generous we give others our time, talents and gifts freely.

"**True generosity** is an offering; given *freely* and out of **pure love**. No strings attached. No expectations. **Time and love** are the **most valuable** possessions you can share." - Suze Orman

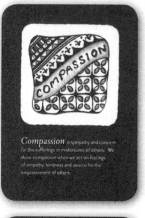

Compassion is sympathy and concern for the sufferings or misfortunes of others. We show compassion when we act on feelings of empathy, kindness and service for the empowerment of others.

"Love and compassion are necessities, not luxuries. Without them *humanity* cannot survive." - Dalai Lama

Gentleness is responding sensitively and peacefully to others cues. When we are gentle with others we show consideration and care for their feelings and physical well-being.

"Nothing is so **strong** as **gentleness** and nothing is so **gentle** as **real strength**."
- Ralph W. Sockman

Contentment is the ability to be satisfied with what we have and who we are. When we are content we are at peace with ourselves and we are free of jealousy and greed.

"The world is full of people looking for *spectacular happiness* while they *snub contentment*." - Doug Larson

Humility is the quality of having a modest and unpretentious view of our importance, ideas and abilities. When we are humble we are able to accept others ideas and recognise the good qualities and deeds of other people.

"There is no respect for others without *humility* in one's self."
- Henri Frederic Amiel

Integrity is an adherence to moral and ethical principles. We show our integrity by being true to ourselves and our values.

"The greatness of a person is not in how much *wealth* they *acquire*, but in their *integrity* and *ability* to *affect* others positively." – Bob Marley

Mindfulness is the quality or state of being conscious or aware of something. When we are mindful we can be fully present in each moment by focusing our awareness on the present moment, while calmly acknowledging and accepting our feelings, thoughts, and bodily sensations.

"With mindfulness, you can establish yourself in the *present* in order to touch the *wonders* of life that are available in that moment." – Nhat Hanh

Initiative is showing creativity through actions that follow the trust placed in us by others. We display initiative by being ready and able to think creatively, solve problems and take risks.

"*Initiative* is doing the right thing without being told." – Victor Hugo

Optimism is a disposition or tendency to look on the favourable side of events or conditions and to expect the most favourable outcome. When we are optimistic we see the glass as half full (and the other half was delicious).

"*Always look* on the bright side of life." – Monty Python

Kindness is consideration and compassion for other living beings. We show kindness when we act with empathy and respect for others.

"*Kindness* in words creates confidence. Kindness in *thinking* creates profoundness. Kindness in *giving* creates love." – Lao Tzu

Patience is about waiting and having confidence in a positive outcome. When we are patient we are able and willing to suppress restlessness or annoyance when confronted with delay. We work with quiet, steady perseverance and diligence.

"*Patience* is not simply the ability to wait - it's how we *behave while we're waiting*." – Joyce Meyer

Love is an overwhelming feeling of affection. Unconditional love means we love someone without judgement and we show our love through thoughtful acts of kindness.

"*Love* is all you *need*." – The Beatles

Peacefulness is firstly a state of self which accords mutual harmony between people or groups, especially in personal relationships. When we are peaceful we are present, mindful and empathetic towards people, places and things.

"*Everything* we do is *infused* with the energy in which we do it. If we're frantic, life will be frantic. If we are peaceful, life will be peaceful." – Marianne Williamson

Playfulness is the state of being full of high-spirited fun. We demonstrate playful qualities when we engage in fun activity and share in the joy and laughter of others.

"We don't stop playing because we grow old; we grow old because we stop playing." - George Bernard Shaw

Tact is skill and sensitivity in dealing with others or with difficult issues. When we are tactful we are being honest in a kind and sensitive way. We keep our words soft and sweet in case we have to eat them later.

"Tact is the art of making a point without making an enemy." - Isaac Newton

Reliability is meeting expectations to which we have agreed. We demonstrate reliability when we are honest in our intentions, deliver on our promises and honour our commitments.

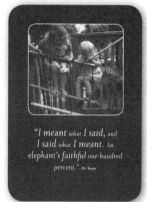

"I meant what I said, and I said what I meant. An elephant's faithful one-hundred percent." - Dr. Seuss

Trust is having confidence and reliance on the integrity, strength and ability of another person or thing. When we are trusting we courageously expect others to act fairly and with integrity.

"Trust is the glue of life. It is the most essential ingredient in effective communication. It is the foundational principle that holds all relationships." - Stephen Covey

Resilience is the ability to recover readily from adversity. We are resilient when we can maintain our positivity and optimism in difficult times or circumstances.

"Persistence and resilience only come from having been given the chance to work through difficult problems." - Gever Tulley

Wonder is to be filled with admiration, amazement, or awe. It is the enjoyment of something we don't necessarily understand. When we are full of wonder, we exercise our curiosity and delight in the natural beauty of life.

"Wisdom begins in wonder." - Socrates

Respect is the key to relationships. When we show consideration for another person, we communicate to them that they are valued. Feeling valued contributes to a sense of trust and self-esteem and is reflected in the individual's ability to form and maintain relationships with others.

"A person's a person no matter how small." - Dr. Seuss

Available at:

www.childspace.co.nz

Appendix 2:
Further resources available

Respect – a practitioner's guide to calm & nurturing infant care & education

"What a most welcome book this is! Toni has provided a readable and practical guide for early childhood teachers interested in respectful practices with our very youngest citizens: babies." Dr. Carmen Dalli

"This book provides a wonderful example of linking theory to practice. Through her detailed observations and captivating photographs, Toni Christie breathes life into the concepts of respect, free movement, and primary caregiving." Dr. Paula Jorde Bloom

$20.00

For multiple copies: **$16.00 each for an order of 5 or more copies; $12.00 each for an order of 20 or more copies.**

Leadership & management for early childhood education

This comprehensive resource will save you from re-inventing the wheel. With over 20 years experience in managing early childhood centres we have put together a guide for centre directors, managers, supervisors and head teachers. It includes philosophy of leadership and management, simple guidelines for ensuring your centre meets regulations and legal requirements, example job descriptions, induction procedures, simple templates for various necessary documentation and much more. A great resource which will benefit centre managers, leaders and administrators.

$30.00 or $20.00 for electronic copy

Example policies for early childhood education

Updated annually, this example book of policies will help when you are writing or reviewing your early childhood centre policies. You will find a policy for everything you can think of and perhaps a few you haven't!

$20.00

Performance appraisal, teacher registration & mentoring

This resource contains a hard copy of the templates used for performance appraisal and teacher registration. A disk of the templates is also included so they can be easily transferred for immediate use in your setting.

"Teacher appraisal is a very sound evidence-based process. It incorporates a comprehensive support programme for provisionally registered teachers where appropriate. Clear guidance is given to teachers as to what is expected of them. The process includes self reflection and comments from the centre manager on the registered teacher criteria and a six-monthly meeting with the principal. Goals are set and rewards for achievement negotiated. The process is positive and supportive and promotes improvement in teaching practice and career development."
Education Review Office.

$30.00 or $20.00 for electronic copy

Self review: simple steps to quality improvements

This resource contains a hard copy of the framework used for self review at Childspace. Examples of the framework in action are included as is a disk of the electronic template.

"Self-review systems are well implemented and highly effective. A wide range of guiding documents creates an interlinked framework for review at both management and centre levels."
"Self review is embedded in staff practice, is well implemented and informs ongoing positive changes to the programme and environment. The process is inclusive and consultative and reviews are very well documented." Education Review Office.

$30.00 or $20.00 for electronic copy

Contact us:

Childspace
Early Childhood Institute

Resources and prices accurate at the time of publishing and may be subject to change.

(04) 461 7076 phone, **institute@childspace.co.nz** email
www.childspace.co.nz

Values cards

The 32 values we hold most dear include respect, love, trust, playfulness, compassion, kindness, joy, integrity, initiative, honesty, loyalty, resilience, service, grace, optimism, reliability, gentleness, patience, peacefulness, wonder, generosity, excellence, enthusiasm, creativity, contentment, beauty, humility, mindfulness, gratitude, courage, tact and empathy.

Each card features an original illustration and definition, images specific to early childhood and quotes from the likes of Dr. Seuss, The Beatles, Bob Marley and Monty Python. Each pack is contained in a gorgeous cotton drawstring bag as pictured. We use these cards for writing children's learning stories, at team meetings, for display, in discussion with children and for parent education.

$24.00 per pack
Or **$20.00 for orders of 10 or more packs**
Or **$14.00 for orders of 20 or more packs**
Also available electronically for insertion directly into learning stories and documentation **$15.00**

The Space magazine

The Space magazine is a practical, fun, full-colour glossy magazine published especially for teachers and parents of young children. With lots of photographs, practical activities, regular columns on parenting, science, art, food and nutrition, this magazine is a must for every early childhood service. The Space has published feature articles and interviews with well respected international early childhood experts as well as reviews, stories, ideas, recipes, child friendly jokes, projects and photographs from teachers here in Aotearoa/New Zealand and around the world.

There are 4 issues per year and subscribers can specify single or multiple copy subscription. Subscribers receive generous discounts on all professional development courses and conferences. Contact us directly for pricing of subscriptions for multiple copies: accounts@childspace.co.nz

$60.00 annual subscription

Values posters

These posters are all on glossy A2 lightweight card and feature original illustrations capturing teaching and leadership values.

$8.00 each or ANY 3 for $20.00 (+ postage tube)

Leadership in ECE institute

This comprehensive institute will be delivered over one evening and one full day. Participants will benefit from networking with other leaders in early childhood and will enjoy sharing valuable knowledge and experience. Subjects covered will include an overview of leadership, communication, teambuilding, conflict, administration, performance appraisal, teacher registration, mentoring and whole centre review. Register additionally or separately for the follow on centre tours the next day. **Visit www.childspace.co.nz to register for this annual event.**

Keynote Speakers

Toni and Robin Christie are inspirational Keynote speakers in the field of early childhood education. Toni and Robin Christie founded Childspace Early Learning Centres and subsequently the Childspace Early Childhood Institute in Wellington, New Zealand. They began their careers in early childhood with a small centre in their own home and have both taught early childhood for various ages and contexts.

Currently their work involves teaching adults about the importance of the early years. Toni and Robin have written books and resources, they publish a quarterly magazine, hold annual conferences, design and build environments for children, inspire early childhood practitioners through their keynote and workshop presentations, and they love their jobs!

Toni and Robin believe that early childhood is the most significant stage of every person's development. They are driven to provide practical, relevant, natural and aesthetic resources and environments for all who play and work with very young children. They have applied their talents throughout New Zealand and Australia as well as other parts of the World such as Canada, The Cook Islands, Denmark, Germany, Fiji, Ireland, Malaysia, Mexico, Scotland, India, Singapore and the United States.

Appendix 3:
Index of quotes

Appendix 4:
Index of ideas